Stress Management Workbook

TECHNIQUES AND SELF-ASSESSMENT PROCEDURES

Sandra E. Gramling · *Stephen M. Auerbach*

Virginia Commonwealth University

PRENTICE HALL, Upper Saddle River, NJ 07458

© 1998 by PRENTICE-HALL, INC.
A Pearson Education Company
Upper Saddle River, NJ 07458

10 9 8 7 6 5 4

ISBN 0-13-853920-0
Printed in the United States of America

Contents

Part Four

Stress Management for Specific Populations and Problems   120

Preface

Why and How to Use This Workbook

Stress management workbooks usually follow a "cook-book" format which present the reader with a smorgasbord of stress management techniques with little guidance regarding what techniques might be most useful or what is the best way to try to learn and practice the stress management techniques. This stress management workbook is different. We take a skills training approach to the acquisition and application of specific stress management techniques. This means that you can learn the stress management skills presented here just like you learn any other skill. Learning to reduce your stress level is like learning to play an instrument or sport. You will become better able to manage your stress with practice. The fundamental stress management exercises presented early in the workbook will become second nature to you with practice. The more specific and complex stress management techniques presented later in the text build on these fundamental skills. Rather than a "cook-book" approach, we view our book as taking a flow chart, or building block, approach to help you identify those stress management techniques that might be most useful for the stressful situations of concern to you. The idea here is to program sufficient flexibility into the workbook to allow you to tailor a stress management program to your own particular stressors.

This workbook is designed to complement the companion textbook <u>Stress Management</u> (Auerbach & Gramling). While the main text emphasizes the theoretical and conceptual foundations of stress and stress management, the workbook offers skills training in stress management embedded in the same conceptual framework articulated in the main text. It is not necessary to use the textbook to understand and use the techniques presented in this workbook but the text would give you far more background and context for the application of the various stress management techniques presented here.

You will find that the workbook will help you identify the situational determinants, or "triggers" of your stress response. Understanding how the situation influences your stress response will help you select the stress management strategies that will be most useful for you. Well established learning principles are incorporated into the workbook to maximize your ability to learn and apply these stress management techniques. For example, procedures such as shaping, goal setting, overcoming roadblocks, and self-monitoring, which are known to enhance skill acquisition, are used throughout the workbook. These procedures will help you acquire specific stress management skills as well as monitor and track your progress.

We have written this text in what we hope you find to be an interactive and engaging style. We have included numerous "stress" cases drawn from the classroom and our clients to illustrate the use of the various techniques. Throughout the workbook you will beencouraged to interact with the text by completing simple written and experiential exercises that are more fun than work.

The specific skills are presented in a pyramid format. The exercises presented in Section I are the most general and most fundamental of all the stress management exercises. These exercises provide the foundation for all of the rest of the exercises presented in the workbook. Learn the principles and actual exercises presented here and practice them so that they become second nature to you. The basic skills presented in Unit II form the next level of the pyramid, these are the basic building blocks of stress management. Sections III and IV incorporate different aspects of the building block skills learned in Sections I and II. You can branch out in Sections III and IV to build a stress management program tailored to your particular situation and your particular form of the stress-response. Give these techniques a try. Stress relief begins on the following pages.

First a word of thanks to the hundreds of students who have passed through our Stress Management class in recent years who have provided feedback on earlier versions of this workbook. Also, special thanks to the graduate student teaching assistants and undergraduate interns who provided feedback and helped draft selected sections of earlier editions of this book. Special thanks go to Steve Schwartz, Revonda Grayson, Rob Nicholson, Carol Lakatos and Anne Meyers.

Sandra E. Gramling
Stephen M. Auerbach

Part One

Fundamentals of Emotion-Focused

and

Problem-Focused Coping

Chapter 1

HELP! I'm All Stressed Out

If you are reading these words you are probably interested in learning how to better manage your stress. Stressors which may be impacting you right now may have occurred in the past, be ongoing in the present, or be events that you are anticipating in the future. Let us introduce you to some ideas that can *HELP YOU RIGHT NOW* to think about and respond to your stressors more adaptively.

The Key to Adaptive Coping

The key to coping adaptively with stress is learning to tell the difference between those stressors you can control from those stressors you cannot control. There are different stress management techniques for these two different types of stressors and we cover both types in this workbook.

● Stressors You Cannot Control

Many people generate a great deal of physical and emotional tension trying to change or manipulate events that are out of their control. For example some people find driving very stressful and get extremely upset when other drivers are inconsiderate, or simply do not drive the way the way they think they should. The first author saw a client for therapy once who would become infuriated every day on his ride home from work in rush hour traffic, partly because the other drivers would speed and he thought that was wrong, and partly because cars would be illegally parked in the far lane of the busy thoroughfare he drove each day. He reported that he would get so mad that he would frequently race up behind the illegally parked cars (which were unoccupied) and then swerve back into an open lane at the last moment because he "wanted to teach the car owners a lesson." After some reflection he could see that his coping strategy could have no influence on the owners of the illegally parked cars and probably had no influence on the parking behaviors of other drivers in traffic with him. Now this is an extreme, but still a very real example, of how sometimes people can get all stressed out (and do things that may be dangerous or at a minimum nonproductive) by something over which they have absolutely no control. We can all think of examples where we have gotten ourselves all worked up over something we could not control.

Do you get upset in traffic when other drivers speed or go too slow? Do you get irritated when other drivers stay in the passing lane continuously but do not even drive the speed limit? Does getting upset do anything to help the situation? No, and in fact negative emotion often feeds on itself and leads to more negative emotion.

◆   <u>Emotion-Focused Coping</u> is Effective for Uncontrollable Stressors

Just because you cannot control a stressor does not mean that you have to let the stressor control you. If you learn to regulate your emotional response to events, then you have control over your stress response rather than the stressor. In the driving example, do you want to let the other drivers determine your emotional state, ruin your day, give you a headache? The key point in emotion-focused coping is that while you might not be able to control the stressor, you can learn to control your stress response.

> Examples of Techniques that can be Effective Emotion-Focused Techniques Include:
> - Deep Breathing
> - Progressive Muscle Relaxation Training
> - Visualization

Learning to control your emotional and physiological responses when the uncontrollable stressor is the behavior of others does not mean that you have to agree with or condone that offensive behavior. Learning to regulate your emotional and physiological responses is simply a way for you to gain control over your emotions and physiological responses rather than letting the situation or other people control you. You will find these techniques are very useful in situations where you get anxious or upset over the behavior of others that you cannot control. Just as importantly, these techniques are useful in situations where "stuff" happens (there is a more popular and colorful "S" word that you may want to substitute for "stuff") that you have no control over at the moment (e.g., your car breaks down, bad weather, a course is not offered that you need to graduate) that thwarts you from reaching some goal. These are the easiest to learn and most fundamental of all the coping strategies covered in this workbook.

●   **Stressors You Can Control**

Some stressors can be influenced or changed to make them less stressful. That is, with some of the stressors you face, direct action on your part could reduce the stressfulness of the situation. This is particularly true of interpersonal stressors where it is the behavior of other people that you find stressful. Some people get stressed because they take on too many responsibilities because they can't say "no." You may find yourself stressed because your parents still treat you like a child. Another example would be the stress many people experience when teachers, supervisors, or other people in authority seem insensitive to the needs and feelings of those people they oversee. Assertiveness skills and social skills training are both aimed at teaching people skills to directly and effectively interact with other people in ways that maximize the possibility of successful (stress reducing) interactions. Similarly, the people who are chronically stressed because they always overbook their schedule, or those who are stressed because they procrastinate can learn to manage their time better in order to reduce their stress level. This would mean *doing* things differently, and that's what we mean in this workbook when we discuss direct action techniques or problem-focused coping strategies.

♦ <u>Problem-Focused Coping</u> is Effective for Stressors That You Can Change or Influence

Dealing with some stressors "simply" requires good planning. Financial planning prior to the holidays is an example, or developing a good study plan so that you are not cramming for finals at the same time you are trying to prepare for the holidays. Of course if good planning was simple, we would not be stressed out by it. The key to good planning is to break things down into small steps and give yourself credit, some sort of tangible reward or verbal praise, for each small step you accomplish. As we mentioned above, problem focused skills are also important for managing interpersonal stressors. Many people do not try to change interpersonal stressors because they are worried about how the other person will react or what other people will think. Sometimes we need to work on changing our thinking before we can use some of the problem focused skill building techniques below.

> Examples of Techniques that can be Effective Problem Focused Techniques Include:
> - Assertiveness Training
> - Time Management
> - Social Skills Training

● Stressors Do Not Cause Stress: The Stress Response is the Result of How You Interpret the Stressor.

A test does not make you anxious, your boss does not make you angry, the traffic does not get you all "stressed out." We often think and talk about stressful events as if they cause us to feel a certain way or behave in certain ways, but that's really not the case. It's really what the stressor means to us, how we appraise it, that determines how stressful we find a situation. For example we teach a class in stress management and we have observed the entire spectrum of emotional responses to test grades. The interesting thing is that we observe this wide range of emotional reactions among students who get the same grade. One student gets a "C" and is jubilant, another student gets a "C" and is angry, another student doesn't care, and another student is anxious. They are all being exposed to the same stressor, a "C," but the reactions are different because a "C" means different things to these different students. For many it is an assault on their self-esteem. A "C" is interpreted as a negative event. Other students are more than happy to take their "C" and run. Their self-esteem is not tied up in school work. They do not interpret a "C" as threat to their self-esteem. These different reactions to the same event, a "C," is an example of differences in cognitive appraisal. Each of us has accumulated a different set of life experiences and have different learning histories. Therefore, we respond to life events through our own individual and unique belief system. The proof that it is our *appraisal* of the "C" and not the grade itself that leads to our emotional response lies in the fact that if "Cs" *caused* stress, everyone who received a "C" would be anxious, yet many people are happy with a "C." If we believe that getting excellent grades is important, then tests are more likely to be associated with anxiety. Remember, it is not the test or the grade that causes anxiety and distress, its how we interpret the meaning of them to ourselves that determines how anxious we become.

◆ Cognitive Coping Strategies

Cognitive Coping Strategies are used in both emotion and problem focused stress management techniques. Sometimes we need to re-examine maladaptive beliefs such as "I must be perfect" that contribute to our stress ("perfectionists" are frequently stressed because they are trying to meet an unobtainable criterion). Sometimes we need to use our thoughts to help motivate us to take action and try a problem focused intervention on our stressors.

> Examples of Cognitive Coping Strategies Include:
>
> - Changing Maladaptive Beliefs
> - Stopping Unwanted Thoughts
> - Stress Inoculation Training

In this workbook we will cover a range of stress management techniques that you can learn and incorporate into your daily living to manage stress. The central themes of the workbook, including the role of cognitive appraisal as a precursor of the stress response and the broad categories of coping strategies (emotion focused and problem focused strategies) are introduced. In general, emotion-focused coping techniques (emotional regulation techniques) are most effective when the person has little control over the stressful situation and problem focused coping (strategies which involve attempts to directly influence the stressor rather than one's emotional response to the stressor) is most adaptive when the individual has some control over the stressor. Most of the stressors experienced by people in the course of daily living have mixed features, that is, aspects over which the person has little control and aspects which are changeable. The fundamental techniques of emotion and problem focused coping presented in Chapters 2-3 are the most essential skills you will need to improve your ability to manage the stressors in your life.

Chapter 2

Deep Breathing Exercises ☺:
The Fundamental Emotion-Focused Coping Skill

Background

Deep breathing exercises are one of the essential building blocks to mastering relaxation procedures of all kinds. They are one of the easiest and most efficient methods for eliciting the relaxation response. If you only learn one skill from this workbook, this is the one to master. You want to practice this technique and learn to apply it in stressful situations so that it comes to you naturally, like "second nature" in stressful situations.

Virtually everyone can benefit from deep natural breathing. It is especially helpful for people who are prone to panic attacks, fatigue, hyperventilation, headaches, muscle tension, anxiety, and cold hands and feet. Often these disorders are the result of poor oxygenation and waste product disposal, although a combination of factors may contribute to individual cases. Regardless of the cause or the specific nature of distress, deep breathing is an exceptionally cost-effective strategy for managing stress levels in the short term. That is, deep breathing provides you with a technique you can use any time or place to manage the immediate emotional and physiological arousal associated with stressors. After the deep breathing exercise is well learned you will probably want to use it in conjunction with techniques that will help you change the nature of the stressor itself.

Take a moment right now to examine how you normally take a deep breath. Put one hand on your upper chest and the other on your abdomen. Now, take a deep breath and notice which hand rises first. If your top hand rises first, you are using a chest or thoracic breathing pattern. If the hand over your abdomen rises first, you are using an abdominal, or diaphragmatic breathing pattern.

Chest or thoracic breathing is a shallow pattern of breathing that many people adopt over time without even realizing it. This type of breathing is often rapid and irregular and associated with anxiety and emotional distress. Shallow breathing can diminish your ability to cope with stressful situations, as well as contribute to panic attacks, anxiety, headaches, and fatigue. The deep breathing exercise that we recommend is intended to give you control of your physiological responses when confronted with stressful situations. If you can learn to lower your level of physiological/emotional arousal by a few notches you will be able to think more clearly and more successfully apply other coping strategies to stressful situations. Remember, even when the stressor is uncontrollable, you can still control your emotional response to the situation if you learn coping strategies like the deep breathing exercise.

Deep Breathing Exercise

It is best to breathe through the nose if possible. First, find a comfortable position with your eyes closed. Place one hand on your chest and the other on your abdomen. Try breathing normally initially, focusing on how your chest and abdomen rise and fall. Do they feel well coordinated? Is there tightness or rigidity? Scan for tension in the throat, chest and abdomen. When you first practice this exercise focus on breathing in so that the hand over your abdomen can feel the air first, followed by the rising of your chest and shoulders. This exercise may seem a bit unnatural at first, but it will become more automatic and soothing with practice.

Deep Breathing Exercise

1. Begin by sitting or standing up straight in good posture while remaining comfortable.

2. Breathe in slowly through your nose.

3. As you inhale, first fill the lower section of your lungs. Your diaphragm will push your abdomen out to make room for the air and the hand over your abdomen will rise. Continue to inhale and feel the middle part of your lungs expand as your lower ribs and chest move forward slightly to accommodate the air. Finally, feel the upper part of your lungs expand as your chest raises slightly and your shoulder rises and you feel your hand placed beneath your collarbone rise. Draw in your abdomen slightly to support your lungs. This slow deep breath can be completed in a few seconds as one smooth, continuous inhalation.

4. Hold your breath for a few seconds.

5. As you exhale slowly through your mouth, pull your abdomen in slightly and lift it up slowly as the lungs empty. When you have completely exhaled, relax your abdomen and chest. Let the tension out of your shoulders.

6. At the end of an inhalation phase, raise your shoulders and collarbone slightly so that the very top of your lungs are sure to be replenished with air.

Practice Now

Go ahead and breath very deeply and very slowly, filling your lungs from the bottom to the top just as we described above. Let your shoulders rise and hold your breath for a few seconds and then exhale slowly through your mouth. Let your abdomen and chest relax and let the tension out of your shoulders. Don't try to do it perfectly. Try it once to see how it feels, look over the instructions again and try it again. Ideally, if one hand is on your abdomen and the other is on your upper chest, you will be able to see your abdomen hand move first as you inhale and then the hand on your chest. Try it several times this way until you can easily force the air into the lower part of your lungs first when you inhale. If you practice this exercise you will probably be doing it correctly. Remember, you do not have to do the exercise perfectly to benefit from it.

Homework

Note that for this exercise to be effective, you do not have to breath this way all the time, but you do need to be able to take three deep breaths like this when you want to. Most people need to practice this exercise in order for them to feel comfortable with it and to be able to do it without effort when they need to. Initially, it is best to practice deep breathing when you are <u>not</u> particularly stressed. Deep breathing will be an excellent way to relax once it has been paired with the state of deep relaxation. For now though, we just want to practice so that the breathing is easy and natural. You want to practice in a variety of different situations and postures (e.g., at home and work, sitting and standing, working and resting, etc., so that you are comfortable doing the exercise anywhere.).

Goal Setting and Overcoming Roadblocks

An ideal goal for practice would be take about forty-five seconds, 5-6 times a day, and take three deep slow breaths the way we described above. For most people this "homework" is not seen as very difficult. Most people enjoy the exercise and most think that they would have the time to be able to practice. The most frequent difficulty people have in actually practicing, is remembering to practice. To help yourself remember to practice you might want to pick a few set times a day (e.g., just before meals, before every class, when you wake up and just before bed) or a few specific situations (e.g., whenever you get in the car, whenever you turn on the TV). Planning a few set times to practice every day is a good way to get started on this exercise. You may also want to put a post-it note up someplace where you would see it frequently to remind you to breath or place a note in a drawer that you use frequently as a reminder.

Tracking Your Progress

Keep a tally sheet of how many times you practice the deep breathing exercise. You will find that by keeping a record you will be more motivated to practice and more likely to remember to practice. Many people keep a 3x5 card with them with the date for each day of the week on each row and place a hash-mark next to the date for each time they do the breathing exercise. The following page presents an example of a simple recording sheet.

There are several strategies you might want to consider to help you remember to practice the exercise. One technique is to schedule the exercise into your daily routine to coincide with other routine events in your schedule. For example, many people decide to practice when they first wake up, at breakfast, lunch and dinner, and just before bedtime. Since these events occur during the day anyway, they can serve as reminder, or a cue, to do the breathing exercise. Another strategy is to put "sticky notes" with the word "breath" in conspicuous places to act as a reminder to breath. You want to develop your own strategy to remember to practice and soon the deep breathing habit will be virtually automatic.

Deep Breathing Recording Sheet

Date	Number of Times I Practiced Breathing Exercise
4-15-97	/ /// /
4-16-97	// / / /
4-17-97	/ (weekend- forgot until I went to bed)
4-18-97	// / / // (made a point to remember today)
4-19-97	// / ///
4-20-97	/ // // / //
4-21-97	/ // / /// / (practicing is easy; do it all the time)
4-22-97	/ // / / /// (did deep breathing in tense situation at work - really helped me calm myself before I took my test)

You do not have to use a 3x5 card to keep track of your breathing exercise. You can use a notebook, or an appointment book, or anything that you find makes record keeping convenient. The important point is to come up with a system that works for you.

Self-Efficacy Beliefs

Self-efficacy beliefs refers to how confident a person is that they will perform adequately in a particular situation. These beliefs predict a person's actual performance in a given task. Take a moment and assess your own self-efficacy beliefs regarding these exercises in the box below.

Self-Efficacy Rating

How confident are you that you will be able to practice this exercise 4-5 times a day?

On a scale of 0% confidence ...to..... 100% confidence what rating would you give yourself?

Write your rating in here _____.

If you gave yourself a rating of 80% or more you will very likely be successful. For most people, when they figure out how to remember to practice, they have no difficulty with this assignment and are on their way to developing one of the most powerful, yet most portable and easiest stress management techniques available. If you have read this book thus far you are almost certainly one of those on their way to success. If you gave yourself a rating of less than 80% but want to learn these stress management skills, go back and see if the goal was set too high for you. If a less ambitious goal of 3-4 times per day or even 2-3 times per day increases your confidence rating, then start with a smaller goal and build yourself up to the more challenging one. It is always better to set smaller goals and progress slowly than to have goals that are too high and lead to failure. Set yourself up for success. Set goals that are realistic and reachable.

Deep breathing is the fundamental exercise you can use to regulate your emotional and physiological responses in stressful situations. We will be using the deep breathing technique throughout the workbook. In just a few chapters you will learn a relaxation procedure called progressive muscle relaxation training. Deep breathing is the first part of the relaxation exercise. You will find that the breathing exercise will give you even more power to control your emotional and physiological responses to stressors once it is paired with the relaxation technique. Because we will be using deep breathing so frequently throughout the workbook, we are going to give it its own symbol ☺ to indicate that you should take three deep breaths and let the tension out of your shoulders just as we have described in this chapter. Sometimes we just use the symbol ☺ and sometimes we will use the symbol ☺ with the phrase "breath slowly and deeply, and each time you exhale let the tension out of your shoulders."

Chapter 3

Self Assessment: A Fundamental Problem Focused Skill

Background: Figuring Out the Problem

Practicing the deep breathing exercise from Chapter 2 will give you control over your physiological and emotional responses in stressful situations. The second fundamental stress management skill to learn is self assessment. Self assessment means learning to identify the situations associated with the stress response, learning to measure your own stress response in these situations, and figuring out what it is you do, or don't do, when in these stressful situations that makes things better or worse for you. Basically, self assessment is going to involve you being a detective and you are going to be investigating yourself. The investigation is going to require you to study yourself in different situations, observe how you respond and quantify some of your emotional and behavioral responses when stressed.

Self assessment is a problem focused skill because you need to make a plan for collecting information about stress and you need to problem solve any difficulties that come up when you try to implement your data collection plan. You need to engage in overt instrumental behavior to accomplish this task (i.e., you have to write things down, you need to take written notes not just mental notes). This might sound too much like work but its easier than it sounds. Throughout this chapter we will provide you with examples and recording forms that will make information collection relatively painless. Start by taking a few minutes to jot down the stressors in your life that you think you would like to manage better.

Some people seem to be stressed out all of the time but when they look at their day more carefully they find there are some situations in which they feel much worse and some situations much better. This is important information when developing a stress management plan that is right for you. Other people know exactly what kinds of situations are likely to be associated with increased stress but don't have a clue as to what to do about it. Whether you feel like you are too stressed out to even know where to begin, or if you feel like most of the time you manage your stress well and its just certain situations that give you trouble, the simple tracking procedures that are presented in this chapter will be helpful.

Start by simply describing some of the important aspects of the top five stressors in your life right now. Remember, stress is the past, the present, and the future. Think about each of these types of stressors as you formulate your list. Note both the controllable and uncontrollable features for the stressors you identify. Jot down all the details that come to mind as you consider what the sources of stress are in your life. You might end up changing your list later, but for now keep your thinking broad as you consider what stressors you find most problematic. You can include major life events as well as chronic background hassles, things that bother you from the past as well as fears you might have about the future. Give this a few minutes of thought and then go ahead and fill out the table on the next page.

My Top Five Stressors

Describe your stressors. What features of are controllable? Uncontrollable? Is the stressor something that already happened, something happening in the present, or something you are anticipating in the future? Is the stressor a major life event or a chronic daily hassle? Describe yours stressor in detail.

1._____

_____

_____

2._____

_____

_____

3._____

_____

_____

4._____

_____

_____

5. _____

_____

_____

Now that you have described your stressors and noted some key features of each, what do you need to do next to learn to manage them better? You need to learn about the ABCs of stress.

The ABCs of Stress

Stress has a past, a present, and a future. That is, remembering past events, dealing with the present situation, or thinking about what may happen in the future can cause many of us worry, anxiety, anger, guilt, depression, sleeplessness, or a whole host of other stress reactions at any given moment. How often have you been sitting in class or at work and found yourself suddenly feeling anxious or angry because you were thinking about an argument you had yesterday or the presentation you have to give next week? None of us are capable of living entirely in the present moment. Learning the basics of stress reactions is one of the fundamental steps to learning more about ourselves and discovering how we cope with life.

The phrase "ABC's of stress" refers to more than simply "the basics." It also refers to the specific events that can trigger or maintain stress reactions. The stress response does not occur in a vacuum. That is, feeling stressed is generally tied to specific situations. Assessing the events that surround stress reactions can facilitate your understanding of the situational determinants of the stress response and help give you insight into your patterns of coping. The "ABCs" refer specifically to Antecedents, Behaviors and Consequences. Antecedents are events or situations that trigger stress reactions. Behaviors reflect the stress response itself, that is, the *thoughts, feelings and actions* that you experience when stressed. Consequences are the events that follow A and B. Simply knowing "what happened next" can provide insight regarding why you react the way you do in certain situations. In examining the ABCs the first thing most people can describe in at least a general way is the B, what they do, feel, or think when stressed. For most people it is the B that leads them to read a book like this to learn new coping strategies. They do not want to *feel* anxious, or *avoid* certain situations (*actions*), or *think* and ruminate constantly about past traumas or future apprehensions.

Perhaps you already have a broad range of coping skills and wonder whether much of this will be useful to you. Consider the following case of Susan, a successful well adjusted business woman who came in for the treatment of chronic neck and facial pain:

> Susan married at the age of 19, had one son, and divorced two years later. Her ex-husband later committed suicide, leaving her to raise their son on her own. Susan remarried at the age of 26, however, her second husband was an alcoholic and severely abused her. She again divorced two years later. For the past eight years since the second divorce, she returned to school and continued to raise her son on her own. At the time Susan came in for treatment, she was in a long-term relationship with a wonderful man, loved her job, and had just been to her son's high school graduation. Her son was going to attend a nearby university and she was pleased that he would be on his own but not too far from home. However, chronic neck and facial pain that had begun eight years prior continued to bother her.

13

> *Doctors diagnosed the pain as stress-related. Susan felt confused and angry; she believed that she had coped very well with traumatic events in her life and could not understand why she should be suffering from a stress-related pain problem at this point when things were going well. Susan's therapist recommended that she keep a <u>structured diary</u> in order to gain insight into her daily activities. Daily record-keeping revealed that many "little things," or daily hassles, accumulated throughout Susan's day. Through record keeping, patterns were revealed. Together, Susan and her therapist agreed that while she coped very adaptively to major life stressors, she did not cope as well with minor events. As a result, chronic low-level stress kept her body in a state of high physiological arousal, leading to her pain problem. A comprehensive stress management program including daily relaxation exercises greatly reduced Susan's pain and improved the quality of her life.*

Many people feel that they have coped well in the past with major stressors, and resent being told they are suffering from stress when nothing terrible is happening. It is possible to suffer from stress-related troubles from average daily living. Why? There are several reasons for this. Major stressors such as family death or natural disasters are made public. In these cases, others recognize and understand the high levels of stress being confronted by the suffering individuals. People often pull together to help. Social support can be a great stress reducer. The individual under stress recognizes the source and may modify his or her behavior to help cope with the strife. For example, taking a few days off from work, seeking out social support through family, friends or counseling, and making time to care for yourself are all common positive ways of coping with major (and minor) life stressors.

However, major life stressors do not occur with high frequency for most people. For many people, daily hassles can pile up to cause or worsen chronic stress. Minor life stressors, or daily hassles, do not make such a striking impact as major events, and many people do not exhibit the same preparatory or recuperative coping behaviors when dealing with the everyday stress. Daily hassles often do not elicit offers for social support as readily as major life events. In addition, many people do not recognize daily hassles as sources of stress to seek help for. Nevertheless, daily hassles can build up and result in stress-related physical disorders and psychological distress.

The key to self assessment is to observe yourself. Written records help to discover patterns, as it did in the case of Susan. Written records can also help make you more aware of events and your own behaviors in daily life. Taking a little time to record your thoughts, feelings and/or behaviors can help you gain valuable insight into troubling areas. Even record keeping alone can help modify your behavior. For example, individuals who write down everything they eat in a day will lose an average of five pounds without deliberately trying to modify their diet! Why is this? Many people are not aware of how much they really eat, smoke, clench their teeth, bite their nails, etc. Many of these behaviors have become habitual, and are performed without complete awareness on occasion. Record keeping helps draw attention to these behaviors. Awareness is the first step in behavior change. The following sections will detail these very important beginning stages of a behavior change program: defining the target behavior and record keeping.

Defining the Stress-Related Behavior You Want to Change

Self assessment begins with clearly identifying the B you want to target for change. The first step in reducing your stress is to choose a goal and specify the behaviors to be changed to reach that goal. Review your list of top five stressors. Are you still comfortable with this list? Add additional stressors now if you want. Take your final list and prioritize them in terms of the severity of each stressor. Put your stressors in order with your most severe stressor (causes you the most distress, has the most negative impact on the quality of your life) to the least severe, least problematic of your stressors. Now that you have them in order from most to least distressing put a plus sign (+) by those that you want to work on and a minus sign (-) by those that you think you would rather not deal with at this time. For example, you may find your smoking behavior is associated with a great deal of stress because those around you hassle you all the time about it. Besides being hassled for smoking you may also want to quit because you are worried about your health. However, you might decide that you do not want to deal with this problem now smoking if smoking is one of your coping strategies to help you calm down and relax. In this example you may want to wait and tackle smoking after you have worked on reducing your stress in other areas.

Take each of your stressors with plus signs and make them more specific by describing the problem as a *behavior-in-a-situation*. In other words, to define the problem as specifically as possible you must place it in its environmental context. A common goal that many people who read this book will have is "I want to be less anxious." This is a great goal and you're on the right course (or in the right course if you are reading this book as part of a class) by reading this book. Now, let's make the goal more specific; let's tailor the goal to your particular circumstances. Let's specify the problem as a *behavior-in-a-situation*. Use the form below to specify your goal as a behavior in situation. In what situations do you experience the stress response that you are seeking to change. Provide details about the situation and the stress response (what you think, feel, and do or not do) when stressed. Fill in this table (make it longer if you want) giving the details of the situations in which you feel stressed and the thoughts, actions, and feelings that are associated with being stressed in that situation.

Stress Response (Behavior) Occurs in Specific Situations

Situation = Antecedents   Thoughts, Actions, Feelings = Behavior

Stressor =Test Anxiety- Before and during exams. Usually starts 24 hrs before test. Worse when I study alone.	Thoughts: "I'll Fail"; "I'll never learn all this" Actions: Can't study; pacing, fidgeting Feelings: apprehension, nauseous, tense

15

If you are having trouble coming up with concrete details in the table above, here are some hints to help you specify your goals clearly:

(1) Make a list of precise examples of the problem. For example, "I eat too much" is too vague a statement; "I eat too many cookies" or "I eat too much when I watch television" are more specific examples of the problem.

(2) Listing details of the problem. List details of a problem often improves problem solving skills. For example, assume that the target goal (the stressor or behavior) is to reduce anxiety in social situations. You might list that you avoid contact with friends who always gather to socialize after a particular class, or that you feel particularly uncomfortable when you walk into a room alone where other people are already socializing. Once you note the details of the situation, you can target these particular areas to help control the overall goal.

(3) Observe yourself. If you have some general ideas about when you get stressed and how you respond when stressed you can get more detail by observing yourself in a stressful situation. Notice the details of the situation and how you feel, think, and react in the situation. If you are trying to increase a behavior that you presently are engaging in at a very low rate or not at all (e.g., studying, assertiveness, relaxation, exercising) then also observe what you are doing *instead of* what you want to be doing. For example, if you are trying to increase exercise, you may observe that you generally watch TV during times of the day when you could be exercising.

Even if your goal is not a specific behavior, behaviors will need to be altered in order to achieve that goal. For example, if it is your desire to decrease a chronic pain condition (not a behavior in itself), then you would specify a behavior or series of behaviors that will lead up to that ultimate goal--in this case, perhaps you may want to institute a program of regular progressive muscle relaxation, deep breathing, visualization, and maladaptive thought reduction. These are the specific *target behaviors* that will lead to the ultimate goal, the reduction of pain.

Selecting a Stress Management Goal

If you are like most people you have filled in the behaviors in a situation table with 4-8 different behaviors in a situation. A typical person may have details about test anxiety, a particular phobia, anxiety in dating situations, unwanted pressure from parents, feeling time pressured, uncertainty about the future, and difficulties dealing with authority figures. For each of these problems the hypothetical person has gone through steps 1-3 and provided details in order to describe the problem as a behavior in a situation. Now that you have a good handle on the specifics of your stress related problems where do we go from here? You need to decide which problem area to work on now. Of course its your decision regarding where to start. Below are a few things to consider when selecting a stress-related problem to target for change.

(1) Most people do best targeting a problem area of moderate intensity and difficulty. It is important to pick a problem that is sufficiently distressing so that you are motivated to learn new skills and apply them in your daily living. However, you do not want to start with something that is so distressing and complex that you risk getting frustrated and give up early because of slow progress.

16

(2) Many people have several sources of stress in their lives at one time. Its OK to continue to cope with some of these problems as best you can while using this workbook to learn skills to address the specific problem you select.

(3) Review your list and see if you do not already see patterns in your stress-related situations. Perhaps several of the items on your list reflect assertiveness problems, or time management problems. If that seems to be true you may want to group the items together that seem to fall under one of the interventions discussed later in this book (e.g., assertiveness training, time management, study skills training) and then select the area you want to target.

(4) On occasion people have difficulty finding any stress in their lives with which they are not already coping well. If you are one of the fortunate few, then use this workbook as a stress prevention book. Whether we are stressed at the moment or not, all of us face the prospect of finding ourselves in stressful situations that exceed our capacity to cope. You can use this workbook to learn the fundamental and building block exercises from sections 1 and 2 as a "protective" set of skills for a time when the stressors you experience are more serious than they are right now.

Look at the later chapters and consider whether any of these techniques might be helpful to you in the future. For example, in running stress management groups for medical students the first author found that the most frequently cited stress management deficiency prior to the program was time-management skills. The vast majority of the medical students report that although they were very busy as undergraduates, they basically felt that they were pretty well organized and pretty smart and coped just fine with the time demands of the pre-med curriculum as well as their other time commitments. However, they found medical school to be a completely different story. There is simply not enough time to learn everything and do everything you are supposed to do at the level of mastery you are accustomed to achieving. The medical students responded very favorably to the cognitive interventions and time management interventions outlined in this workbook. Their only lament was that they did not acquire these skills before they started medical school.

Tracking Progress: Basic Record Keeping

You have a specific goal in mind. Now you need to learn to track and quantify your stress in the specific situation(s) you have selected. In order to modify your actions, you must first know what you are doing, literally. We perform have become so natural to us that they are performed without conscious realization.

Consider the case of Susan, introduced in an earlier section:

> *Susan spent most of her work day sitting at her computer. While working intently, she was completely unaware of various extraneous behaviors she was engaging in: often her jaw and shoulder muscles were taut and she would tap her teeth together. Similar behaviors were occurring during the drive home, and while she was engaged in various hobbies such as sewing. At night, Susan would grind her teeth. Eventually, Susan's dentist noted signs of dental wear and prescribed a bite guard to minimize the damage caused by the continual grinding.*

As in Susan's case, many people with chronic facial pain often engage in a variety of oral habits (e.g., teeth grinding, lip biting, jaw clenching). Often people with facial pain do not realize that they engage in these oral behaviors with such great frequency until the pain develops or the dentist tells them that their teeth show evidence of wear from grinding. Night bruxing, or grinding your teeth in your sleep, is another example of how you can unconsciously engage in behaviors that are stress related. You cannot be any more unaware that you are performing a behavior than when you are asleep. Therefore, the first step in changing a behavior is to learn exactly what it is that you do and in what context. In order to accomplish this step you need to observe yourself and take notes--the more detailed the better. Pretend that you are a behavioral scientist observing a subject; take note of what actually occurs. In other words, don't just guess about what you do; studies have shown that casual assessments about our own behavior are often inaccurate. When you record every instance of the behavior as it happens you may find that the behavior occurs a lot more--or a lot less often-- than you thought it did. For example, many people with chronic jaw pain grind their teeth, bite the inside of their mouth, or engage in a number of other oral habits that cause the facial muscles to be tense. Most facial pain sufferers do not notice that they are engaging in many of these activities. Keeping track of the number of times the teeth are clenched using a wrist counter can help the pain sufferer notice how often he or she engages in this habit. As mentioned previously, awareness of behavior is the first step to planning strategies for behavior change. The remainder of this section will explain ways in which you can keep records of your behavior.

Structured Diaries

A structured diary is an elaboration of the behavior in a situation table you filled out in the beginning of this chapter. You use a structured diary to obtain even more detail about the situations in which you become stressed, the nature of your stress response, and importantly the events that follow the situation and your response in that situation. Clearly, this is not the kind of diary in which you write down random thoughts, concerns, or wishes before you retire at night. Instead, we want you to record events that occur before and after the target behavior as it occurs throughout the day. As soon as you notice that a relevant behavior is occurring (or has occurred), make note of it and also note any events that happened before (antecedents) and after (consequences). As you write, try to answer the questions: Who? What? When? Where? and Why? Describe the situation, what you were thinking, feeling or doing, and what others were doing. Try to make an entry as soon as the behavior occurs; trying to reconstruct the event later may overlook important details that could have uncovered identifiable patterns.

Date Antecedents Time	Behaviors-Actions, Thoughts, Feelings	Consequences
When did it happen? Who were you with? What were you doing? Where were you? What thoughts and feelings were you having?	What thoughts did you have? What types of emotional and physiological feelings did you have? What actions were you performing (or avoiding)?	What happened as a results? Was it pleasant or unpleasant? Were there short and long term consequences (e.g., yelling in anger may bring immediate relief, then guilt)

The example below are excerpts taken from the structured diary from a client who is suffering from stress-related chronic facial pain:

Structured Diary of Stress-Related Facial Pain

Date Time	Antecedents	Behaviors-Actions, Thoughts, Feelings	Consequences
Monday 7:30am	Driving to work, Traffic is really bad, accident on the freeway	Grinding my teeth, holding tight to the steering wheel. "I'm going to be late!" Feel anxious	Felt a tightness in my jaw, pain starting in the back of my neck. Ignore the pain.
Monday 11am	Boss handed me a Pile of work and said to have it done by lunch	Grinding my teeth, chewing my nails, want to say something to boss but keep quite instead.	Angry with myself for not being assertive. Pain in jaw gets worse. Take two aspirins.
Monday 6:30	At home alone watching TV	Chewing my nails thinking "why am I doing this, I do not feel stressed"	Noticed nail biting and stopped
Monday 8:00pm	Still watching TV Spouse says something critical	Bit my lip but did not say anything. Feel really angry. Think "he has no place criticizing me"	Noticed I was biting my lip but could not stop I was so angry. Jaw hurt later and mad at myself later for not saying anything

Subjective Units of Distress

You can rate the intensity of feelings using Subjective Units of Distress (SUDS). SUDS ratings can be any coding system you choose: 0 to 10, 1-100, -3 to +3, etc., to record the intensity of a feeling (e.g., emotions, pain). For example, assume you are trying to assess your anxiety level. You could use a numbering system from 0 to 10 to indicate how anxious you felt at a given time.

0-----1-----2-----3-----4-----5-----6-----7-----8-----9-----10

no   moderate   extreme

anxiety   anxiety   anxiety

The following is an example of a record keeping plan using SUDS ratings. This individual is trying to assess his feelings of anxiety to see how the intensity fluctuates in different situations.

Time	Rating	Comments
Breakfast	1	Woke up feeling OK
Lunch	4	Had trouble starting the car and was late to work/school
Afternoon	6	Failed a test at school
Bedtime	8	Was a bad day, ruminating over everything that happened, feel hopeless and tired but real anxious at the same time. Can't sleep.
Breakfast feel	6	Woke up and felt a little better than when I went to bed but still anxious. If I fail this class I'll be put on probation.
Lunch	4	Met with a friend for lunch, she didn't do well on the test either, didn't feel so stupid or alone anymore
Dinner	2	Professor gave a huge curve and I didn't do as bad on the test as I had originally thought. Wish I hadn't ruined a whole day and night worrying

SUDS ratings are also very helpful when used in the structured diary format. You can use SUDS rating to rate the intensity of any emotion, urge, physiological sensation etc. Sometimes its useful to rate two different aspects of a stress-related problem at the same time. To illustrate this, the following is an excerpt from the previous facial pain example. We asked the client to rate her level of anxiety in the Behaviors column and the intensity of her pain in the Consequences column.

Date Time	Antecedents	Behaviors-Actions, Thoughts, Feelings	Consequences
Monday 7:30am	Driving to work, traffic is really bad accident on the freeway.	Grinding my teeth, holding tight to the steering wheel. "I'm going to be late!" **Anxiety SUDS = 4**	Jaw muscles feel tight, pain starting in the back of my neck. Ignore the pain. **Pain SUDS = 3**
Monday 11am	Boss handed me a pile of work and said to have it done before lunch	Grinding teeth, chewing on nails, want to say something to boss but keep quiet instead. **Anxiety SUDS = 7**	Angry with myself for not being assertive. Pain in jaw gets worse. Take two aspirin. **Pain SUDS = 5**

The following page includes a blank sample structured diary. You may want to make copies of this page for additional use, or modify it to more closely fit into your lifestyle.

SAMPLE STRUCTURED DIARY

Date Antecedents Time	Behaviors-Actions, Thoughts, Feelings	Consequences
When did it happen? Who were you with? What were you doing? Where were you? What thoughts and feelings were you having?	What thoughts and feelings did you have? What actions were you performing?	What happened as a results? Was it pleasant or unpleasant?

Advanced Record Keeping: Frequency and Duration

The structured diary is very helpful to discover patterns of behavior and the events that may trigger and maintain the behavior. But some stress management plans require the observation of how often and/or how long the behavior occurs as well. Consider the following examples of people trying to stop smoking:

> *Charles began a stress management plan to quit smoking. While a structured diary helped Charles to become more aware of the situations in which smoking occurred (in the car, at kitchen table, when tense at work), the behavior occurred with such great frequency that he was unable to keep up a continual structured diary. Charles began carrying a 3 x 5 card with him and made a hash mark each time he smoked a cigarette. Once Charles had learned the crucial information regarding the situations in which he smoked from his structured diary it became much more efficient for him to track his progress with the frequency count method. Using this method he discovered that smoking occurred with much greater frequency than he had originally thought. He also found that it was very rewarding for him to be able to count and graph his progress during his stress management intervention.*

> *Amy was a 26 year old smoker when she decided to quit. She would buy several packs at a time, and learned through her structured diary that she most often smoked while at work as a waitress. Amy believed that other wait staff were "bumming" cigarettes from her packs while she was not around, because she often had less cigarettes left at the end of the day than she believed she had smoked. However, when Amy began keeping a frequency count by tallying the number of cigarettes actually smoked, she was surprised to learn that she smoked more than she thought throughout the day.*

For the previous two examples, a **frequency count** was the simplest way to achieve the recording goal. Frequency counts simply involve keeping track of the behavior as it occurs. In the case of the pen chewer, Charles noticed from his structured diary that smoking occurred most in the car, at kitchen table, and when tense at work. He kept a 3 x 5 card in his pack of cigarettes and simply made a mark every time he noticed an instance of pen chewing. **Duration** of the behavior is another method of data collection that may be appropriate depending on the target behavior. For example, if you are trying to increase the time you spend with your kids in positive interactions, you may want to record time in minutes of the same behavior (e.g., playing a game together), as well as time spent interacting in a negative manner (e.g., arguing). Or if you are trying to increase the amount of time that you walk for exercise, you may want to record in minutes how much time you spent walking each day/week.

You need to experiment with record keeping to find the best way to record your particular target behavior. Some people keep a copy of their structured diary with them at work/school and make notes throughout the day as the behavior occurs. Others put a record sheet on their refrigerator, bedroom mirror, bathroom wall, etc. Some find that it is easier for them to keep notes in their daily calendars or appointment books. A special small pocket notebook is helpful for some. Others have devised more creative methods to record the frequency of behaviors while in situations where it is difficult to make notes (e.g., social situations). Some people put buttons/pennies/dried beans in one pocket and transfer one of the items into the other pocket when they notice that their target behavior occurred. The number of items are then tallied and recorded on a chart later. This particular form of record keeping can be performed unobtrusively (i.e., other people don't notice that you are keeping track of your behavior). Some individuals who are trying to reduce cigarette smoking find it helpful to record the number of cigarettes in a pack when they begin the day and the number remaining in the pack at the end of the day. Wrist counters may be helpful in recording frequency counts of a behavior. Exactly *how* you keep records is not important: The key to success is to make it accurate yet simple enough to fit into your lifestyle.

Depending on the behavior that you are trying to modify and your environment, a variety of record keeping strategies can be employed. If you find that your present method of record keeping is not working, then experiment with other techniques. No one technique works best for everyone in every situation. Remember, you may need to be creative to find a method of record keeping that is appropriate to your target behavior and lifestyle.

Homework

Keep a structured diary of your behavior in a situation for one week. Under B make sure you include your thoughts, actions and feelings. Think about how to best quantify your stress response (frequency, intensity, duration). Make sure you include details of the consequences as well. After one week of conscientiously keeping your structured diary, review what you have written and look for patterns in the situations and patterns in the consequences. Tinker with your recording procedures if you are not keeping up with the diary as well as you would like. You need to find a way to remember to keep your diary and to make keeping the diary something you can do as part of your daily routine.

Overcoming Roadblocks

1. Keep records in writing. People are unable to keep track "in their head." The first time you put your notes in writing will make it easier to put them in writing the second time and so on.

2. Make notes as the behavior occurs or as soon after as possible. Memory recall of one's own behavior is not always accurate.

3. Try to be strict in counting and include all (or as many as possible) instances of the target behavior. However, if what you are targeting happens so frequently that it would take too much time to record every instance, pick certain times of the day to record for a set period of time.

4. Keep your method of data collection as simple and incorporate it into your usual routine.

Part Two

Basic Skills to Change

Feelings, Thoughts, and Actions

Chapter 4

Lowering Arousal and Changing Negative Emotion

Background

In 1929, Edmund Jacobson published a book entitled <u>Progressive Relaxation</u>, in which he proposed that the body responds to stress with muscle tension. In turn, this tension increases anxiety and stress and an escalating cycle begins. He proposed that muscle relaxation decreases tension and is incompatible with anxiety. Joseph Wolpe, a behavioral psychologist, introduced the idea of **reciprocal inhibition**. Reciprocal inhibition is a the technical terminology to describe the concept that one can't be both relaxed and tense at the same time. Wolpe proposed three activities that were relaxing and incompatible with tension: sex, eating, and relaxation exercises (unfortunately only relaxation exercises have received serious study--they won't let us run the sex study at the university despite having many willing undergraduates).

Rationale

There are many different types of relaxation techniques that could be covered in this workbook. Meditation, yoga, and biofeedback, for example are all good relaxation techniques. We will cover another relaxation technique, visualization, later in the workbook. However, we use progressive muscle relaxation training as our building block relaxation technique because it has some features that make it especially useful in producing relaxation. First, its easy to learn the relaxation procedure on your own, which is not true of many of the other forms of relaxation. However, the most important feature of progressive muscle relaxation exercises is that these exercises physiologically induce relaxation in the muscles. In progressive muscle relaxation training you will tense and relax various muscle groups in sequence. When you tense a muscle (for example clench your fists tightly) and hold the tension the muscle becomes fatigued. When you release the tension the muscle relaxes, but because you fatigued the muscle by keeping it tense for 30 seconds or so, when you release the tension the muscle becomes even more relaxed than it was before you tensed the muscle. If we attached sensors to your skin we could measure the activity of the underlying muscle and have a direct measurement of the lower level of tension in your muscle after tensing and releasing. This is what we mean we say that progressive muscle relaxation physiologically induces relaxation.

The figure on the next page illustrates the changing levels of tension (dotted line) in your muscle before you tense (original baseline), during tension, and after you relax the muscle (new baseline). Focus your attention on the muscles of your right hand and forearm and note the amount of tension you feel. Now TENSE these muscles by making a fist and hold that tension for about 30 seconds as you notice what the tension feels like. Now RELAX all at once and let your arm fall to your lap. Notice the reduction in tension. The level of tension in the muscles of your right hand and forearm have just changed in the same pattern illustrated in the figure on the next page. Namely, by creating tension in the muscles, you have fatigued the muscles, and physiologically induced relaxation such that the level of tension is now LESS than it was before you started the exercise.

Changing Levels of Muscle Tension as You Tense and Relax

ORIGINAL RELAXED BASELINE

\--

TENSE DELIBERATELY

\---

                                                 RELAX

NEW BASELINE

\---------------------

Many people suffering from tension and anxiety have a difficult time at first becoming aware of the tension in their muscles. This exercise insures that the muscles become more relaxed and the remainder of the exercise is focused on increasing awareness of the changing levels of muscle tension created by tensing and releasing. The state of relaxation induced by the tensing/releasing exercises described later in this chapter is very pleasant and enjoyable, which is good of course, but that is really a pleasant side benefit of relaxation training. The ultimate purpose of relaxation training is to (1) pair the breathing exercise with the deep state of relaxation produced by progressive muscle relaxation exercises, (2) focus attention on the different sensations created by tensing and releasing the muscles so that *in everyday activities you will be more aware of rising levels of muscle tension*. Rising levels of muscle tension will become a cue, or signal, to you to ☺ take three deep breaths, filling your lungs from the bottom to the top and as you exhale let the tension out of your shoulders and other muscles. The point is to develop a powerful, portable tool, that will allow you to relax when you want and need to. In day to day situations you will not get as relaxed as you will when you are going through all the muscle groups. You will simply bring your level of emotional and physiological arousal down several notches and give yourself more control over your body and emotions.

Increasing Awareness of Bodily Tension

Many of us are not sensitive to muscle tension changes and only notice them when tension reaches very high levels. Moreover, certain muscle groups are more difficult to detect when tension levels are high. For many people these vulnerable muscle groups become so conditioned to being tight that the muscles remain taut for long periods of time. The muscles eventually become chronically fatigued, and soreness sets in. Elevated levels of tension is the culprit behind many types of headache, facial pain, sore shoulders, stiff necks, and backache.

One of the most important things to learn with PRT is to be more sensitive to the signals your body is sending you and apply relaxation exercises **before** the level of tension becomes excessive. In order to become more sensitive it is important to pay close attention to the sensations of tension of relaxation. These exercises serve in part as discrimination training so that rising levels of muscle tension in day to day activities come to serve as a cue that you need to step back and allow your body to relax. Recognizing signs of tension is one of the first, and most difficult, steps in the process of stress management and pain prevention. However, a little time invested will pay off in the long run. With practice, you should be able to sense tension very early in the cycle and implement progressive relaxation or deep breathing to reduce the tension. The environment (home, car, work, etc.) will not matter.

Learning plays a very important role in the process of relaxation training. As you practice the relaxation exercises, pair deep breathing and the word "relax" (or "calm," "quiet," etc.) with the feeling of relaxation. Eventually, if the pairing occurs often enough, the paired word (e.g., relax) will elicit the sensation of relaxation without actually going through any more of the exercise than the deep breathing. The mechanism by which this process works is termed **classical conditioning.** Eventually, you should just be able to say "relax" and experience a decrease in your tension.

Relaxation exercises are useful anytime you feel aroused by stress or anxiety. Once you are physically relaxed, you can make better use of cognitive strategies to deal with the stress or anxiety. Progressive relaxation is a way to break the cycle of the stress response. Relaxation exercises and deep breathing are two of the most important and efficient stress management tools you can have in your toolbox of coping skills.

Nine Muscle Groups

There are nine main muscle groups that will be included in this relaxation exercise: (1) hands and forearms, (2) upper arms, (3) forehead, (4) eyes, nose, and cheeks, (5) jaw, chin, front of neck, (6) back of the neck, (7) upper body, and (8) legs up with toes pointed down (9) legs up with toes pointed up. Read through the following descriptions of the procedures, experimenting with tensing the various muscles described before attempting the entire exercise. The first time you read through the muscle groups just practice tensing and relaxing the muscles one by one. After you have practiced just tensing and relaxing the muscles try the whole procedure. When you are ready to try the real thing, don't worry about doing the exercise exactly as it is discussed in this section. Try to be familiar enough with the nine muscle groups that you do not need to open your eyes and check the book. The sequence below is the recommended sequence, however, if do them out of order you will not turn to salt. Read through the whole chapter once before you begin so that you can assess your levels of tension before and after the exercise.

Before You Begin

A few things to remember as you practice the relaxation exercises.

1) Never tense a muscle to the point of pain. You want to get the muscle noticeably tense but never tense to the point of pain. If a muscle group is in pain before you start the exercise, for example a sore neck, sore back, facial pain, be especially cautious. Tense the affected muscle very gently, see how it feels and proceed if the tense/release sequence makes it feel better. If tensing the muscle makes the pain worse, stop. Go to a different muscle group. The relaxation you produce in the other muscles will eventually generalize to the muscle group that is chronically tense.

2) Always make the contrast between tension and relaxation as distinct as possible. When you release the tension, release it all at once.

3) Throughout the exercises pay attention to the contrast in the sensation of tension and relaxation. If you find your mind wandering during the exercise, bring your attention back to your muscles.

4) Do not fall asleep during the exercise. You want to learn to be able relax when you want to during your day to day activities. You do not want to use this technique to learn to fall asleep (Although PRT is an important part of many treatments for insomnia)

Relaxation Procedure

When you begin the exercise, turn the lights down or off. Initially, make sure you are in a place where you will not be disturbed for at least 20 minutes. Find a comfortable position, preferably one that will allow your head to be supported. A reclining chair or bed are good examples. Your only goal during the exercise is to create tension and relaxation in each muscle group and notice the contrast between the two sensations.

First, settle back as comfortably as you can and close your eyes. Start by taking in a few deep natural breaths ☺. Use the deep breathing technique that was discussed in the previous chapter. Focus on your breathing. Tell yourself that breathing and relaxation are the only things you need to think about right now. Clear your mind. Everything else you're worried about or have to do today can wait until you are done. Let this be your time. Give yourself permission to take the time to relax and enjoy the sensations of relaxation you create.

Relaxation Exercises

(1)   The first muscle group to work on is your hands and forearms. With your thumbs on the outside, make a fist with your hand. At the same time, twist your arms around to create tension in your forearms. Notice the tension in your hand and forearm. Focus in on this sensation of tension you are creating in your hand and forearm. Now, all at once, relax your hands and forearms. Let the tension flow out. Notice the difference between the sensation of relaxation you feel in your arms right now and the sensation of tension that you created just moments ago. Focus on this difference. Take a deep slow breath ☺.

If you find yourself becoming distracted, just bring yourself back to the relaxation exercise by focusing on your breathing.

(2)   Next are the muscles of your upper arms. Push your elbows back into your chair until you feel tension in your upper arms. Don't push in so hard that you cause pain, but just enough to cause tension. Focus in on the tension in your upper arms. Now, all at once, let the tension out and relax. Notice the difference in the sensation of relaxation you feel now and the sensation of tension you created just moments ago. Focus on this difference. Take in a deep breath ☺. Notice how relaxed your arms and hands feel right now.

The muscles of the face are the next group to work on. This is an area that tends to harbor a great deal of stress-related tension. The facial muscles are divided into 3 groups.

(3)   The forehead area is a good place to begin. Keeping your eyes closed, raise your eyebrows up as high as you can. Feel that band of tension across your forehead. Focus on that tension, the tension that stress can create. Now, all at once, relax your eyebrows. Notice the difference between the sensation of relaxation you feel in your forehead now and the sensation of tension you had created just moments ago. Focus on that difference.

(4)   Now let's do the eyes and nose area. No one can see you doing this so don't hold back. Shut your eyes tightly while crinkling up and pulling up your nose toward your eyes. Focus on the tension around your eyes and nose and cheeks. Feel that tension. Now, all at once, relax your face. Notice the difference between the sensation of relaxation this area feels now and the sensation of tension you had created a moment ago. Focus on that difference.

(5)   Now, let's do the third area, the jaw area. While biting down on the teeth in the back of your mouth, try to pull the corners of your mouth down into an exaggerated clown frown (looks like this ☹). Focus on the tension you are creating. Now, all at once, let your face relax. Notice the difference between the sensation of relaxation your face feels now and the sensations of tension you created just moments ago. Focus on this difference. Take in a few deep breaths and each time you exhale let even more tension out of your jaw until it feels completely slack and loose.

(6) The next area to work on is the shoulders and neck. Much tension related to stress is harbored in this area. Pull your chin down into your Adam's apple until it almost touches your chest. Feel the tension you are creating in your neck. Focus on this tension. Now, all at once, relax your neck, let it loose. Notice the difference between the sensation of relaxation you feel now and the sensation of tension you created just moments ago. Focus on this difference. Now, breath very deeply and very slowly ☺ and each time you exhale let the tension out of your shoulders. Let your shoulders drop as all the tension drops away.

If you are uncomfortable with the previous method of creating tension in your neck, try a different method of creating tension in these muscles. Remember, how you create tension is not important. As long as you can feel the difference between the tension and relaxation you are doing the exercise properly. Another way to create tension in this area is to gently pull your head backwards, as if you are dropping it into your neck. Experiment until you find a way to create tension in the back of your neck that works well for you. Remember, never tense to the point of pain.

(7) The mid-body area is next. While taking in a slow breath, draw your shoulders back as if you were trying to make your shoulder blades touch and at the same time arch your back. You should feel tension in your abdomen and chest from holding your breath and tension through your upper and lower back from pulling the shoulder blades back and arching the back. Hold this position and notice what the sensation of tension feels like. Then exhale slowly, letting the tension flow out as you relax. Notice the difference between the sensation of relaxation you feel now and the sensation of tension you created in this area just moments ago. As you breath very deeply and very slowly ☺, notice, and remember the difference between these two sensations. Focus on that difference.

(8) The two final muscle groups involve the legs. First, raise your legs up in front of you, as if you were trying to lift them off the chair (if you are practicing laying horizontal, lift your legs up at about a 45 degree angle). Now, point your toes toward the floor while keeping your legs out in front of you. Feel the tension you are creating in your legs, from your toes to your hips. Focus on this tension. Now, relax your legs and let them fall gently to the floor. Feel the sensation of relaxation in your legs now. Notice and remember what this sensation feels like.

(9) Finally, raise your legs back up and hold them in front of you again. This time pull your toes back towards you so that they are pointing at the ceiling. Feel the sensation of tension that you are creating from your toes to your hips. Now, relax your legs and let them fall gently to the floor. Notice the difference between the sensation of relaxation you feel in your legs now and the sensation of tension you had created in it just moments ago. Focus on this difference. Breathe very deeply and very slowly ☺, let the sensation of relaxation permeate the muscles of your legs and let it spread throughout the muscles of your body.

This completes the tensing/releasing of the nine muscle groups. Keep your eyes closed for a few moments and focus on how your muscles feel at the moment. Scan your muscles and notice any tension that might remain. If you detect any tension, try to concentrate on that area, send messages to this area to relax and loosen and let the tension slip away. You may want to tense and relax again those muscles that did not get as relaxed as the others the first time through the exercise. Twice is enough. Do not expect all the muscles to get relaxed at the same rate. The muscles that are more difficult to relax will eventually catch up as the relaxation from the other muscles generalize. After you have reviewed your muscles in your own minds eye and focused your attention on what the sensation of full body relaxation feels like open your eyes and continue to notice the sensations in your body as you re-orient yourself to the room.

Summary List of Muscle groups

1. hands and lower arms -- make a fist with the thumb on the outside of the fist

2. upper arms -- push elbow into the back of the chair or bed

3. forehead -- arch eyebrows

4. eyes, nose, cheeks -- shut eyes tightly, crinkle nose

5. mouth, jaw, neck -- Bite down gently on the back teeth   make an exaggerated clown frown by drawing the corner of the lips down

6. neck and shoulders -- draw chin into Adam's apple

7. mid body -- take a deep slow breath filling the lungs from the bottom to the top, pull   shoulder blades back and arch the back

8. legs -- lift legs up and point toes to floor

9. legs -- lift legs up and point toes to ceiling

Tracking Your Progress

A great way to keep track of your progress in developing your relaxation skills is to keep a record of tension/stress levels before and after the exercise. Prior to beginning PRT, rate your level of tension/stress. Use a SUDS scale like those described in Chapter 3. On a scale of 1 to 10, with 1 being no tension at all and 10 being as tense as you can get, write down a number that reflects your level of tension. Then reassess your state of tension/stress once you are finished. You may find that with repeated practice, the numbers will drop in greater increments with less time. For example, it is common for beginners to only drop from a 9 to a 6 in tension levels while they are learning the procedures. With repeated practice, the more experienced relaxer can drop from a 9 to a 2, or even 0, in less time. On the next page there is an example of a relaxation recording sheet which includes a place to record your breathing exercises as well. At the bottom of the record sheet is a place for you to write down your weekly goals for the number of times you plan to practice the relaxation exercise (# times/week) and breathing exercise (# times/day).

Relaxation Record Sheet

DATE	SUDS Rating Pre	SUDS Rating Post	Daily Breathing
_____	_____	_____	_____
_____	_____	_____	_____
_____	_____	_____	_____
_____	_____	_____	_____
_____	_____	_____	_____
_____	_____	_____	_____
_____	_____	_____	_____
_____	_____	_____	_____
_____	_____	_____	_____
_____	_____	_____	_____
_____	_____	_____	_____
_____	_____	_____	_____

Use this sheet to record breathing exercises, relaxation exercises or both. **Breathing**: For each day starting with today enter the date and number of times you practiced the breathing exercise that day. **Relaxation**: Each time you practice relaxation enter the date (time would be helpful as well) and your tension rating before the relaxation exercise and after the relaxation exercise.

Tension Rating: 1=no tension....10=most tension imaginable

GOALS: Relaxation _____ Breathing _____

Goal Setting and Overcoming Roadblocks

An ideal goal for PRT practice is 3-4 times per week for about 20 minutes. For most people the biggest roadblock in reaching this goal is trying to find the time to practice. Practicing PRT is harder for people to fit into their daily routine than the deep breathing exercise. Something that may increase your motivation is knowing that you do not need to do the relaxation exercise (particularly the long form we described in this chapter) for the rest of your life. If you practice with some regularity you will get good at the relaxation procedure in three to four weeks and can move to shorter versions that are easier to find time to complete. The shorter versions involve combining muscle groups, for example tensing the arms and legs together, so that you go from 9 muscle groups, down to 7, then 5 until you are able to take three deep breaths say the word relax and achieve a very good level of relaxation. The more you practice, the sooner you will be proficient enough with the relaxation exercise, that you will not have to spend that much time on them.

Chapter 5

Changing Unrealistic Thoughts and Beliefs

Background

In the very first chapter we introduced the idea that stressors do not cause stress. The key word in the previous sentence is *cause*. Clearly our experience of stress is related to specific situations, but the situation itself does not cause our stress. The stress you experience in particular situations is the result of how you appraise or interpret the situation. If there is something about the situation that you believe is a potential threat to your self-esteem or physical well being you will likely feel anxious and stressed when confronted with the situation. If you believe that it is important to do well in school, that teachers and friends think of you as a "good student" you may well feel anxious taking tests. Another person may believe that school is just something you go through to get a degree and experience relatively little anxiety around tests. The two have different beliefs and therefore different responses to the same testing situation.

Most people agree that their thoughts and beliefs influence their response to stressors. Sometime the difficult part is in deciding whether those beliefs are adaptive or maladaptive for you. Some people with anxiety know that their perfectionism (I "must" do well) causes unneeded anxiety. Other people who find themselves angry a great deal may quickly cite that their beliefs that "life should be fair" leads to many instances of anger when things do not turn out the way they "should." You may be a good student who believes that good grades are important for success in life. Many people share that belief. Is it adaptive or maladaptive? For most people most of the time it is adaptive. The belief motivates people to work hard and obtain good outcomes for themselves. How could this belief ever be maladaptive? Beliefs are maladaptive when they lead to extreme emotional and behavioral consequences. If you are anxious, angry, depressed, frustrated, or experiencing any other strong negative emotion that you would rather not be feeling, then you need to look at the beliefs you hold about the stressor, or activating event, in order to change that emotion. The person who cannot function in other spheres of life because of extreme test anxiety probably has maladaptive beliefs about tests and school performance in general. The skeptic might say "but she's getting good grades, she's getting what she wants, how can that be maladaptive?" Its maladaptive because the level of her anxiety is extreme and is interfering with her ability to function in other areas of daily living *that she would like to function better in.* Only the individual can decide if the emotions she or he is experiencing are so unpleasant that they want to change.

The worksheet below will help you evaluate whether your emotional and behavioral responses are adaptive or maladaptive. If you note a high level of emotion in one or more category, or find that your behavior in the situation did little to make the problem better, you would probably benefit from some of the cognitive restructuring techniques described in this chapter.

ARE YOUR EMOTIONS AND BEHAVIORS
HELPING YOU OR HURTING YOU?

Write down an event which happened to you recently which you found extremely stressful.

_____

_____

_____

Indicate how you *felt* and how *strongly* you felt about it by rating your emotional response on a 1 to 10 scale (SUDS ratings). 1= did not experience that emotion and 10=strongest experience of that emotion possible.

_____ angry _____ guilty _____ anxious _____ depressed

Write down what you did (how did you behave)?

_____

_____

_____

Was your behavior helpful? Did it help solve the problem in the short-term?   ____ ____
                                                                                                              Yes No

Did you behavior help solve the problem in the long-term?   ____ ____
                                                               Yes No

Did your extreme feelings help you to think clearly and solve the problem or deal with the upsetting event?   ____ ____
                                                                                                              Yes No

In order for you to think clearly and thus effectively handle stressful situations and solve practical problems, you first have to develop emotional control. **Emotional self-management is a vital key to stress management.**

This first step in emotional self-management is to become more aware of your habitual emotional stress reactions and to understand clearly that they are not helping you get what you want. Once you are motivated to change your emotional and behavioral reactions to situations, you are then ready to modify your thinking.

Cognitive Restructuring

The term cognitive restructuring and many of the ideas presented in this chapter comes from the work of Albert Ellis. Cognitive restructuring simply refers to the process you go through to change your maladaptive, rigid thinking into more adaptive ways of thinking. Albert Ellis was one of the first psychologists to develop a systematic theory and treatment of emotional distress that focused on the influence of one's beliefs in producing stress. Ellis' treatment is called Rational Emotive Therapy and the exercises that follow are based on his work. Ellis uses the term irrational thoughts and irrational beliefs when referring to maladaptive beliefs. We have found that students and clients alike do not like the term irrational to describe their beliefs and Ellis himself has said he would use the term maladaptive if he were starting over today. Ellis (and the authors) make no value judgements regarding people's beliefs. Only you can decide whether you have beliefs that are so rigid and absolutistic that they lead to unwanted emotional or behavioral distress. An important point of this chapter is to make you aware that you can change those aspects of your beliefs that are making you crazy with stress, anger, etc., without losing all those good qualities that you value in yourself.

So many of the facial pain and headache patients that I (SEG) see in therapy are hard working "Type A" individuals. Many of my patients are very concerned when they first come into therapy because they are afraid that stress management will turn them into a coach potato. They like being very active and accomplishing a lot of things in life, and do not want to diminish that aspect of themselves. Many of them are perfectionistic and their perfectionistic beliefs have been adaptive in that they have driven them to very high levels of achievement. Unfortunately, perfectionism can be very destructive because it sets an unobtainable standard. Nobody is perfect and if you have to be perfect to succeed then you will always fail. Somehow your efforts will always fall short of expectations. Often these patients have a very high need for control and are very anxious and frustrated when things do not go as planned, when they have to depend on others rather than themselves, etc. I have seen a lot of people create anxiety and frustration for themselves, not to mention headaches and facial pain, trying to control things that are out of their control. There is nothing maladaptive or irrational with preferring to be in control, with trying to do your best, with preferring that life be fair to you and others. It is when we think in rigid, absolute terms that things "should," "must," "have to" be a certain way that we set ourselves up for emotional turmoil and often self-destructive behavior. How can you change your beliefs so that you keep the most adaptive aspects but reduce or eliminate the negative aspects. The first thing to do is learn to detect unrealistic and maladaptive beliefs.

Detecting Unrealistic Beliefs

Detecting unrealistic beliefs is the first step in changing your beliefs. Whenever you experience anxiety, anger, frustration or other negative emotions, you can find the belief that causes that emotion by looking first at the stressor, or the activating event, that is associated with the strong emotion. Then ask yourself "what do I believe about this stressor that makes me feel this way?"

KEEP A "THOUGHTS DIARY"

Irrational and unhelpful thoughts contribute to emotional problems and can even cause problems. Here's a way to show yourself how closely your own emotions are related to your thinking. Set up some sheets or pages in a small notebook, using this format: Start with a thought diary like the one in the example below. Once you have at least 5-8 examples (more are better), review what you have written in the thoughts column for each example. Now, review the table on recognizing unhelpful, distorted or irrational thinking. Which of the examples of distorted thinking from the table "Recognizing Distorted Thinking" applies to each of the thoughts listed in the thoughts column of your diary? Look for any pattens in your thinking that may be emerging.

Date/Time	Emotions	Situation	Thoughts
.			

Make an entry in the diary each time you experience a negative emotion (feel blue, get mad, feel nervous, etc.). If possible, do it *at the time you are feeling badly.* Also write down a *very* brief description of the situation you are in. Then write as many thoughts as you can "hear" in your own head. Write them just as you think them, without "fixing them up." Here is an example of what someone else wrote:

Date/Time	Emotions	Situations	Thoughts
Monday 8:15	Anxious/Mad	Late for class on a test day; can't find a parking space	"This is not my fault, its not fair. I'll have to take the essay make-up"
Monday noon	Angry/Depressed	Friend would not eat lunch with me She was not sympathetic about my missed test	"A real friend would listen. She's only friendly when she wants something"
Wed 7:00 pm	Feel sorry for my self/ Depressed	Roommate went to movies with friends and did not invite me along.	"I don't have any friends. I'm going to be lonely as long as stay here, maybe as long as I live"

HOW TO RECOGNIZE THINKING THAT IS
UNHELPFUL, DISTORTED OR IRRATIONAL

VERY EXTREME -- You see things in black and white terms. If your *performance* falls short of perfect, you see *yourself* as a total failure. Or you may see yourself as "fabulous" when you do a good thing, thereby setting yourself up for disappointment later.

VERY BROAD -- You generalize beyond the specific facts of a situation, such as "always, never, everybody, nobody, anything, nothing." Or you label yourself or someone else in a very broadly negative way that goes way beyond the poor behavior you started off thinking about (like "bad, stupid, ugly, lazy, incompetent, inadequate, worthless").

VERY CATASTROPHIC -- You greatly exaggerate bad events until, in your thinking, they are full-blown catastrophes. You use words like "awful, horrible, terrible, tragic, the end of the world." You ignore your coping resources.

VERY NEGATIVE -- You notice only half-empty glasses and ignore the positive features in your life. You make unrealistically gloomy predictions about the future as well, using words like "empty, doomed, hopeless.".

VERY SKEWED -- You "find" things that were hardly there -- a hint or a clue becomes important evidence for you. You wear "feelers" for detecting what you expected to find. And if you can't really find it, they you "manufacture" it from whatever is at hand.

VERY UNSCIENTIFIC -- You ignore evidence, while asserting your own "facts." You use your feelings as "proof of something, read the future, guess about someone's motives (without checking it out), and act on the basis of superstition and hearsay. You misjudge what is likely to happen.

VERY POLLYANNA-ISH -- You convince yourself that problems don't exist, or that certain things are not important to you (when they are). You may also deny having feelings of a strong or negative sort, putting a "good face" on things.

VERY SUPER-IDEALISTIC -- You hold romanticized picture of reality. You have beautiful but unrealistic expectations for yourself, parents, marriage, children, love, a profession, your workplace. Naturally, nothing in the real world measures up to this kind of thinking.

VERY DEMANDING -- You insist that things be the way you want them to be -- your own qualities and behavior, others' behavior, the way your life goes. You use words like "should, must, ought to, has to be." You cause yourself tremendous distress by keeping such rigid rules.

VERY JUDGMENTAL -- You condemn yourself and/or other people for their failings. You find fault in many, many things, and your thinking becomes more and more like a series of critical reviews.

VERY COMFORT-ORIENTED -- Your thinking is continually geared to how you can avoid pain and get what you want immediately. Your thinking expresses concepts such as "too hard, I need it right now, I can't stand this."

VERY OBSESSED -- Your thinking follows a single track even when it is not productive. You go over and over an issue in your mind, until it seems to be the only important thing in the world. It could be an obsession about another person, about something you have done (or not done), about approval, love, achievement, cleanliness, or almost anything.

VERY CONFUSED -- The "pictures in your head" don't match the real world, or you sense things are present or happening when they are not. When your thoughts get out of touch with reality, you cannot depend on your perceptions or conclusions at that time.

Disputing and Changing Unrealistic Thinking

The table on Rational vs. Irrational Thoughts on the following page lists many common thoughts that people have in situations they find stressful. Read over this list and the rational thoughts suggested as more adaptive alternatives. Go over your thought diary again. Did any of these irrational thoughts come up in your diary? Can you imagine substituting a thought from the rational column to your own stressful situation?

Rational Self-Management

You can learn to change your maladaptive thinking to manage your emotional and physiological responses the same way you learned to use deep breathing to calm yourself in situations that you had no control over. Rational self-management is the next step in emotional regulation. With rational self-management you will learn to change the beliefs that cause emotional distress. Deep breathing will only help you control the symptoms, rational self-management will help change the source of your emotional distress.

Goal Setting

Ideally you will want to fill out one of the self-management forms at least once a day. As always you want to set a goal that is realistic for your skill level at your own pace. Like the deep breathing exercise you want to practice this exercise until it becomes "second nature" to you. You want to build your skills so that you get so skilled at detecting your maladaptive beliefs that any time you experience strong unpleasant emotions you take three deep breaths and mentally walk yourself through the self-management form.

RATIONAL VS. IRRATIONAL THOUGHTS

Irrational Thoughts that Cause Disturbance	Rational Thoughts that Promote Emotional Self-Control
1. How *awful*.	This is disappointing.
2. I can't stand it.	I can put up with what I don't like.
3. I'm stupid.	What I *did* was stupid.
4. He stinks!	He's not perfect, either.
5. This *shouldn't* have happened.	This should have happened because it did!
6. I am to be blamed.	I am at fault but not to be blamed.
7. He has no right.	He has every right to follow his own mind though I wish he wouldn't have exercised that right!
8. I *need* him/her to do that.	I want/desire/prefer him/her to do that -- but I don't have to have what I want.
9. Things *always* go wrong.	Sometimes--if not frequently-- things will go wrong.
10. *Every time* I try, I fail.	Sometimes--even often--I may fail.
11. Things *never* work out.	More often than I would like things don't work out.
12. This is bigger than life.	This is an important *part* of my life.
13. This *should* be easier.	I wish this was easier but often things that are good for me aren't--no gain without pain. Tough, too bad!
14. I *should* have done better.	I would have preferred to do better but I did what I could at the time.
15. I am a failure.	I'm a person who sometimes fails.

Model of Rational Self-Management

1.   Activating Event. Write down a problem which has happened or may happen in the future which leads you to perform ineffectively and/or experience an extremely negative emotional reaction which makes it harder for you to solve your problems and achieve your goals.

2.   Consequences. Write Down your inefficient behavior and your negative emotional stress reactions which regularly occur in the face of the activating event you described in number one above.

3.   Beliefs. Write down your beliefs (thoughts, actions, self-talk) about the activating event which are maladaptive (not sensible, true, or useful) and which lead to your self-defeating behaviors and emotions.

4. Goals. Write down how you would like to behave and feel about the problems situation the nest time a similar problem occurs.

5. Dispute/Challenge. Write down and practice using rational statements and attitudes which will help you counter your maladaptive beliefs, manage your own behavior and emotions, and enable you to achieve your goals the next time the problem situation occurs.

Rational Self-Management Form

1. Activating Event (What were you doing, Who with, Where, When; Be Specific)

2. Consequences (Negative behaviors and stress emotions)

   My Behavior is:_____

   _____

   My Emotions are:_____

   _____

3. Beliefs (irrational, maladaptive, false, not very sensible thoughts)

   _____

   _____

   _____

4. Goals (How I would like to behave and feel)

   New Behavior _____

   New Feelings _____

5. Rational Beliefs (sensible, true, adaptive statements that will help you reach your goals)

   _____

   _____

   _____

Chapter 6

Direct Action to Change the Stressful Situation

Background

Direct action stress management techniques involve all of our attempts to directly change the nature of the stressor or stressful situation which is associated with our distress. When we try to change the triggers or the antecedents described in Chapter 3 we are using direct action techniques. In the terminology of Lazarus and Folkman (1984), we are using problem-focused coping skills when we try to change the source of our stress and emotion-focused coping skills when we try to change our own response to the stressor. The direct action techniques covered in this chapter encompass a wider range of techniques than would strictly be classified as problem-focused coping skills. These techniques are a toolbox of techniques that you will apply to your particular behavior in a situation to help tailor the interventions described later to your particular circumstances. It will require plannful problem solving on your part to select the techniques of most use for your particular circumstances and therefore we call what you will do in this chapter a form of direct action interventions. But first, let's go back to the traditional distinction between emotion-focused and problem-focused coping skills.

The following well-known simple poem (a favorite in many religious settings and self-help groups such as Alcoholics Anonymous) succinctly illustrates the interrelatedness of emotional and direct action coping techniques. Remembering its simple message may help to recall and assimilate many of the ideas that are encountered throughout this workbook.

> God Grant Me
>
> the **S**erenity to accept the things I cannot change
>
> the **C**ourage to change the things I can and
>
> the **W**isdom to know the difference

Most situations that you will encounter in life involve both controllable and uncontrollable aspects. That is, a combination of problem-focused and emotion-focused coping skills may be ideal in order to maximize your coping abilities and the potential for a positive outcome. For example, holding in anger over unfair treatment at work is harmful to your state of mind and your body. Emotion-focused coping skills such as relaxation and cognitive restructuring are techniques that help you gain control of your own emotional reactions. However, addressing the problem situation directly may also aid in remedying the source of the anger. Problem-focused coping skills such as assertiveness training to express your concerns and ask for fairer treatment from your boss or coworkers may help to alter the situation itself.

However, occasionally situations may arise in which direct action may or may not be effective. For example, a woman in an abusive marriage may gain little by trying to directly alter the source of the abuse (i.e., changing her husband or attempting to be more assertive in interactions with him). In this example, an attempt to directly alter the situation in these ways may result in more negative consequences. Another form of direct action in which she removes herself from the situation using outside support if needed may be a more adaptive alternative.

Consider the following case examples and try to decide whether emotion-focused, problem-focused, or a combination of both would be the more adaptive method of coping.

Case One:

Amy is a college student at a large urban university. Amy dislikes mathematics intensely but must take a course in college calculus as part of graduation requirements. She became anxious when she did not perform as well as she would have liked during her first exam. The second exam is rapidly approaching. Amy has found that whenever she thinks of the upcoming exam she becomes tense, anxious, and has a queasy feeling in her stomach. As a result, she cleans her room, watches TV, or socializes with friends to take her mind off of the source of her distress. The exam is now two days away.

What is the best way for Amy to cope with her situation?

In this case, a combination of problem-focused and emotion-focused coping techniques will benefit Amy. Relaxation training is one method to reduce her feelings of tension when thinking about the math class. Deep breathing, relaxation exercises, and positive coping statements may all help Amy to deal with her test anxiety when actually confronting the stressor--the test itself. These are all techniques to help Amy control her own emotional reactions. Amy can also use direct action or problem-focused coping techniques to directly affect the situation, and by doing so, indirectly affect her emotional reactions. For example, by actually studying for the exam, Amy's anxiety may lessen. Techniques to directly affect the process of studying may be to break the work down into small steps, develop a contingency contract to reward herself for completing each step, and modify the environment so that it would be more conducive to effective studying (e.g., study in a room with no TV, turn off the ringer to the phone, study at a desk with adequate lighting).

Case Two:

John is driving to work in the morning when traffic suddenly slows to a stop. He cranes his neck out the window and is dismayed to see that a string of stopped cars stretches ahead for as far as sight allows. An ambulance and police car speed past him in the emergency lane. It is now 7:45 and he is expected at work at 8:00 for an office meeting. After five minutes the cars ahead of John start to turn off their engines in anticipation of a long wait. There are no exits from the freeway for miles, nor are there any phone booths or stores within walking distance from his position. John's blood pressure begins to rise.

What manner of coping is most appropriate for John?

In this situation, John is practically helpless. The stopped traffic and arriving ambulance suggest that an accident has occurred relatively recently. There is a good chance that the road is blocked and will remain so for some time before cars can begin to inch their way around the mishap. John has no control over the situation; direct action or problem-focused coping techniques are not applicable in this case. In an uncontrollable situation John can always control his own reactions. Emotion-focused coping techniques will help him to effectively deal with the situation in a way that will be most beneficial to him. Deep Breathing, relaxation, and positive-coping statements may help to lower John's rising blood pressure as well as reduce anxiety and worry over arriving to work late.

Rules of Thumb for When to Use a Direct Action Technique

Problem-focused or direct actions sometimes require more "work" (effort) but they often yield the most lasting benefits. There are a number of matters to keep in mind when considering a direct action approach to stress management. In some cases involving interpersonal situations, the potential **consequences of changing relationships** may need to be considered. Deciding beforehand what changes would be satisfactory and what would be considered intolerable as a result of direct actions may be helpful when alteration of interpersonal relationships is the target goal.

Assess your capacity to change the environment. In some cases, the proper tools or skills may not be available to achieve a positive outcome when taking direct action. For example, when an appliance malfunctions, it is NOT advisable to attempt to directly alter the situation without the proper equipment or knowledge necessary to repair the item. In this case, direct action towards changing a source of stress for which the person does not have the necessary skills may turn out to be a very maladaptive method of coping. The unskilled do-it-yourself appliance repairman may cause injury to himself, others or the appliance. Likewise, hitting, kicking, or tinkering with screwdrivers on malfunctioning computers, televisions, and drink machines may also result in undesirable consequences. Take three deep breaths, tell yourself that it is not the end of the world, and use other emotion focused strategies to lower your level of negative emotion. If something is broken and you cannot fix it, and there is no one else around who can fix it, then there is nothing you can do to change the situation other than to regulate your own level of emotional arousal. You can use direct action in the morning and call a repairperson or colleague to help remedy the situation.

Assess skills deficits versus performance deficits. A skills deficit implies that the individual does not have the ability or the skills necessary to accomplish the desired actions. For example, an individual who lacks an understanding of social skills may have difficulty when dealing with people. He or she may act inappropriately in social situations. A performance deficit implies that the individual knows how he or she is supposed to act but anxiety is hindering or interfering with performance. For example, many individuals feel uncomfortable around certain people and stammer, feel tense and anxious, or behave flippantly. The same individuals may be completely comfortable, relaxed, and appropriate around others.

In order to assess for a skills deficit or a performance deficit, ask yourself, Do you have difficulty in all of the situations in question? Or are there some situations in which you behave effectively? For example, if you feel you can express yourself assertively with your spouse but not your colleagues, then a performance deficit is more likely. If you are unassertive in all situations, then a skills deficit is more probable. Different techniques are sometimes required to master performance and skills deficits. Assessing which deficit more accurately describes yourself will be helpful when deciding on the most effective course of action to take. For skills deficits, the intervention necessary is learning <u>what</u> to do; for performance deficits, the most effective intervention is learning to <u>overcome the anxiety in order to do it</u>. Social skills training, assertiveness training, problem-solving skills training, and communication skills training are among the most common of the problem-focused coping interventions.

Techniques That Can Be Used With All Interventions

The ABC model of behavior discussed in Chapter 3 is a relatively simple way to assess behavior and hopefully you have been using a structured diary to monitor your own behavior. Psychologists have used the ABC system for many years to understand both the specifics of the problematic behaviors that clients present with, but also to understand the situational aspects of the problem that serve to maintain the problem. Watson and Tharpe and others have suggested a system for categorizing the various interventions available using the ABC model as a guide. They describe three general categories of intervention: antecedent-based, behavior-based, and consequence-based interventions. Some of these techniques help to control your own emotional reactions (emotion-focused); others help to directly affect the problem situation (problem-focused). The best stress management strategies utilize a combination of these techniques.

Antecedents (A)	Behaviors (B)	Consequences (C)
Altering preceding events that act as triggers for the unwanted behavior	Modifying thoughts, feelings, or actions by substituting desirable alternatives for undesirable acts, or by practicing desirable acts	Altering events that follow the unwanted behavior that help to maintain it. Reinforce desirable actions and don't reinforce unwanted behavior

Managing the Situation: Changing Antecedents

In a previous section it was explained that antecedents, or the events that occur before the behavior, can act as cues or triggers for the behavior. It is important to learn what antecedents cue your target behavior. If you modify or eliminate the trigger then the behavior will be less likely to result. In a sense, you are breaking the sequence by altering the first step. In addition, if you institute an appropriate new cue or trigger then positive behavioral results are more likely to occur.

There are two categories of antecedent based interventions: modifying old antecedents and arranging new antecedents.

Modifying Old Antecedents

Changing the existing behavioral environment can play a big role in the modification of the target behavior. There are four interventions that are based on this idea: avoiding antecedents, narrowing antecedent control, reperceiving antecedents, and changing chains.

Avoiding Antecedents. Often it can be very helpful to simply avoid the stimulus that "sets up" and results in your unwanted behavior. This technique is particularly useful for consummatory behavior. For example, if you are trying to reduce the amount of deserts that you eat before bedtime, do not purchase these items at the grocery store. If you are trying to reduce drinking alcoholic beverages, avoid the bar or liquor store. If you are trying to lose weight and you noted from your ABC diary that overeating most often occurred when eating out at a restaurant, then you may devise a plan where you avoid eating at restaurants until you have lost a set amount of weight. However, some situations cannot be avoided forever. In these cases, avoiding antecedents can be a helpful technique to use until you feel you have control over the behavior using other interventions. For example, once initial control is gained over weight loss, eating in moderation at a restaurant can be resumed, or healthier items can be ordered from the menu.

Narrowing Antecedent Control. Narrowing or reducing the range of situations in which a behavior can occur is a helpful intervention for reducing undesirable behavior. For example, if you are trying to reduce insomnia, narrow the stimulus control of your bed. Except for sex, the only time you should be in bed is when you are tired and preparing for sleep. This narrowing of antecedent control eliminates reading, watching television, talking on the phone, and worrying. If you are unable to fall asleep in 10 minutes then you should rise and not return to bed until sleepy. Most people find this particular strategy very difficult to comply with. However, if the plan is practiced diligently initially, the insomnia problem will be extinguished more quickly. If you are trying to eliminate smoking, a plan where smoking is restricted to only one location (e.g., the back porch) can help to reduce the frequency of the behavior. Once the plan is established, the smoker may narrow the antecedents even more. For example, initially limit smoking in the bathroom, then to the garage, then only on an uncomfortable stool, until finally the behavior can be eliminated entirely.

Reperceiving Antecedents. Changing the way you think about a stimulus can help control a behavior when antecedents cannot be avoided. Reperceiving a situation is a helpful hint for dealing with temptation. For example, when with friends/coworkers who are smoking, focusing on the negative aspects of cigarettes (e.g., yellowing teeth and fingers, undesirable smell) instead of the pleasures of smoking can help to alter the nature of the situation. A dieter who finds him/herself in line at a fast food restaurant could focus their attention on the grease in which the food is cooked and imagine the fat from the hamburger and fries floating throughout their bloodstream and clogging their arteries. Ordering a salad instead would become more appealing in this case.

Changing Chains. Many behaviors are the result of a fairly long chain of events involving the ABC's. Consequences can become antecedents to new behaviors. As chains grow they become stronger and more resistant to change. The goal is to break the links in the chain to alter the events that lead to the undesirable behavior. It is ideal to break the chain in early links, where they are the weakest. There are three hints to help change chains of behavior: pause before responding, pause to record, and unlinking the chain of events.

Pause Before Responding. This technique is especially useful for indulgent behaviors such as drinking, eating, smoking and situations where anger is likely. The idea is to build in a pause where you refrain from the behavior before you respond. For example, dieters may want to build in a two minute pause in the middle of each meal. The same two minute pause could be used by smokers and drinkers before they respond with a cigarette or a drink. During the pause, ask yourself questions such as "Am I really hungry? Do I really need that cigarette? Am I becoming intoxicated?" If a situation arises that makes you angry, pause to think about what to say or take a deep breath before responding.

Pause to Record. Pausing to record a behavior before it even occurs often helps to reduce its frequency. The earlier in the chain of events that you interrupt, the better your chances of a successful plan. Assume that you are trying to reduce the incidence of an anxiety attack. When you notice the first signs that you are becoming anxious, stop to record in your ABC diary your SUDS rating of anxiety and the eliciting circumstances (e.g., you thought about an upcoming event such as a test or presentation). Pausing to record when the initial feelings of anxiety are felt can help to lower the probability that symptoms will progress to a full blown anxiety attack.

Unlink the Chain of Events. Another technique to help change the chain of behavior is to insert an antecedent that leads to a desired behavior. For example, assume you are trying to spend more "quality" time with your children in the evenings. You have analyzed your behavior and you find that you have a daily pattern of coming home from work or school, taking a nap, waking up and eating dinner before watching television until bedtime. Perhaps you could begin an exercise program, walking for example, and insert it right after you come home from work or school. Regular exercise can help you unwind from the stressful day at work/school and give you the extra energy you need to devote to activities with the children.

Arranging New Antecedents

Creating new events that trigger desirable behavior is often a very helpful strategy to a successful behavior change project. There are six techniques based on this idea: initiating positive self-instructions, eliminating negative self-instructions, thought stopping, building new stimulus control, stimulus generalization, and precommittment/programming the social environment.

Initiating positive self-instructions. These are powerful verbal triggers. Have you ever been in a social situation when you felt so nervous that you weren't sure what to do, maybe you felt as though your mind was blank? This technique is designed to develop new and positive self-speech in problem situations. Generate a list of phrases to tell yourself when you encounter a difficult situation--they will help to remind you what to do. For example, right before a public speech you may say to yourself, "relax, take a deep breath, I am prepared for this, smile, speak loudly, and make eye contact."

Eliminating negative self-instructions. Assume that you are back in the example of walking into the social situation and feeling nervous. Perhaps you are aware of thinking "all these people are staring at me, I'll probably say or do something stupid and they will laugh, I should just leave".

These are negative self-instructions and the goal of this technique is to eliminate them. If you tell yourself that you will fail, it just might happen. Replace the negative instructions with the list of positive instructions that were mentioned previously.

Thought Stopping. This is another type of self-instruction that can be used in combination with the previous two techniques. The goal is to "shout" in your mind the word "STOP" as soon as an unwanted or self-defeating thought occurs. Then replace it with a more desirable, self-promoting thought. This works well with thoughts that you are ruminating over. For example, imagine that you have recently ended a relationship and you find yourself depressed and unable to concentrate on your work due to intrusive thoughts about your ex-boyfriend/girlfriend. You may find yourself thinking self-defeating thoughts such as "If only I had done/been ____, then he/she would have stayed with me," "I can't make it without him/her," or "I will never find anyone to love me." These are all negative thoughts that may maintain your feelings of sadness and lack of concentration. As soon as one of these bad thoughts pops into your head, "shout" STOP, and replace it with a list of positive thoughts. For example, "I deserve better, I am better off without him/her", or "I CAN make it without him/her".

Building new stimulus control: the physical and social environment. The idea behind this technique is to control the physical and social environment in order to trigger desirable behavior. This may sound complicated but stated more simply, place yourself in an environment where you are likely to engage in your desired behavior. For example, if you found by observing your usual behavior that the temptation to watch television in the evenings instead of studying was too strong, change your environment to one more conducive to studying. That is, to increase your study time, go to the library. Television watching is unlikely at the library and you are surrounded by others who are studying.

Stimulus Generalization. This technique describes the process by which a behavior that is learned in the presence of one antecedent is also performed in the presence of similar antecedents. In other words, the goal is to generalize desirable behaviors across different situations. For example, if you have become successful at eliminating your nervousness during speeches by initiating positive-self instructions, also try these self-instructions during other social triggers such as at parties or when meeting new people.

Precommitment and programming the social environment. This technique involves arranging for helpful triggers to occur. A contract with yourself may be helpful. Enlisting the aid of others may also be critical to your success. For example, contract with a significant other that they will remind you of your decision to quit smoking when they observe you with a lit cigarette. If you are trying to modify your diet, ask the family grocery shopper to buy low-fat foods.

Managing the Behavior: Behavior-Based Interventions

The previous section focused on triggers to behavior. The following interventions are designed to target the behavior itself. The following eight techniques either help create new desirable behaviors or are behaviors to replace old, undesirable behaviors.

Substituting New Thoughts and Behaviors. The goal is to develop a positive behavior (including thoughts) in place of negative behaviors/thoughts. If you simply eliminate an undesirable behavior without "filling in" with a new desirable behavior, you may be more prone to relapsing back into old patterns.

Distracting Behaviors. The idea is to distract yourself when temptation, discomfort, or pain seems inescapable. For example, chronic pain sufferers may find it helpful to distract themselves from the pain by engaging in normal activities such as talking to a friend on the phone or reading a book. Socializing with close friends prior to giving a presentation may help to reduce anticipatory anxiety and intense feelings of nervousness.

Incompatible Behaviors. This technique is to substitute a behavior that prevents the occurrence of an undesirable behavior. For example, fingernail biters may substitute nail grooming or sitting on their hands when the urge to bite begins. Facial pain sufferers may find it helpful to engage in jaw exercises and then let the jaw "go slack" as incompatible behaviors for teeth clenching.

Relaxation. This technique can be easily learned with practice and is applicable to a variety of different problem behaviors. It is especially helpful for situations in which anxiety is a problem. Relaxation can be achieved by a variety of different methods, including deep breathing, Progressive Relaxation Training (PRT), meditation, autogenic training, or while listening to music or taped relaxation instructions. Experiment with what technique works best for you and your lifestyle. Pair relaxation with a word such as "calm", or "relax". With enough practice, you can condition your body to achieve physiological relaxation by saying your relaxation word.

Imagined Rehearsal. The idea is to vividly imagine yourself engaging in the desired behavior. This technique can help to practice a problem situation or focus on certain aspects of the situation. For example, someone who suffers from public speaking anxiety may imagine themselves successfully going through the steps of giving an important speech.

Modeling. Many people who try to modify their behavior find that they are not sure what they should be doing. The idea for this technique is to learn through the observation of models--that is, watch other people who are doing what you want to be doing.

Assume that you want to increase study efficiency. You observe a roommate while they are studying and note that they study at the same time every day and at the same location, the television is never on at this time, they make flash cards, and outline the textbook. By observing a model, you now have a starting point for targeting behavior change.

Imagined Modeling. This technique is helpful for individuals who have intense anxiety that makes it difficult to imagine themselves engaging in a particular behavior (imagined rehearsal). The idea is to imagine someone else engaging in the behavior. For example, a person with a phobia of bridges who is unable to imagine themselves on a bridge without experiencing severe anxiety may find this technique a helpful first step. Imagined modeling is not necessary if one is able to successfully use real or imagined rehearsal techniques.

Shaping. Perhaps you are trying to incorporate a new behavior into your life, improve an existing behavior, or your goal is difficult to attain when you first start. For example, an obese individual who has not exercised in 10 years may find it discouraging, if not physically impossible, to initially meet his goal of walking 2 miles a day 4 days a week. The technique of shaping behavior can help with these difficulties. The idea is to reward successive approximations of a behavior toward a desired end goal. There are two general rules for shaping: you cannot begin at too low a step, and the steps in between cannot be too small. For example, the obese individual who wants to make a lifestyle change of regular exercise may begin by walking to the end of the neighborhood block. After several successful trials at this level, the individual now walks around the block before they receive a reward. Eventually, the individual walks around the block 2 times before receiving a reward, then three, then four. Gradually the distance and time spent walking is increased until the individual is able to meet their desired end goal of 2 miles a day/four days a week. A steady experience of success strengthens gradually improving performance. The individual is more likely to maintain his end goal (and in this case, less likely to suffer from punishing soreness or injury from too much, too soon).

Managing the Contingencies: Consequence Based Interventions

Behaviors are either maintained or eliminated by the reinforcing or punishing events that follow them. That is, if a behavior is followed by a contingent reward, the behavior is more likely to occur in the future. If a behavior is followed by an aversive state, then that behavior is less likely to occur in the future. Although punishment is one technique to decrease behavior, reinforcement of desirable behavior is more effective and durable in the long run. In other words, punishing yourself for not performing up to your goal will be less effective as a behavior change technique than reinforcing good behavior. Take a look at an example, which plan do you think would maintain study behavior on a long-term basis? (A) "If I don't study 6 hours tonight, then I can't watch any TV tomorrow" (punishment); (B) "For each hour I study tonight, I will allow myself to watch one hour of TV guilt-free tomorrow" (reinforcement). Plan B is less restrictive and helps to break the end goal into small steps of work toward a desired reward. Plan A is likely to create frustration and relapse.

There are two helpful hints for maximizing the reinforcers' effects. (1) The consequences must be contingent upon the behavior, and (2) consequences should follow the behavior as close in time as possible. The following techniques describe several different kinds of reinforcers that are helpful as consequence based interventions: Premack reinforcers, shared reinforcers, tokens, imagined reinforcers, and verbal self-reinforcement.

Premack Reinforcers. Use a high-probability activity to reinforce a low-probability behavior. For example, for many students television watching is often a high probability behavior (i.e., it occurs at a relatively high rate). Studying is generally a low probability behavior (i.e., it occurs at a lower rate than television watching). As in the previous example, use television watching as the reinforcer for studying. For others, socializing or talking on the phone is a high probability behavior. House cleaning, music practicing, number of pages completed by a writer, and exercise, are possible low probability behaviors that can be increased by using time socializing as a reinforcer.

Shared Reinforcers. One technique that combines social support with self-change is the concept of sharing reinforcers. In order for both you and your helper(s) to receive the reward, you must successfully meet your desired goal. For example, contract with a friend/spouse to go out to dinner or to an amusement park on Saturday if you meet your goal of exercise/studying 4 days that week. This technique has two motivating effects: you may feel pressure to stick to the plan because your behavior determines another's reward also, and the support person may help you attain the goal with reminders, keeping the house quiet, exercising with you, etc.

Tokens. Sometimes it is not possible to deliver the reinforcer immediately after the performance of the desired behavior. A token system can be used to help bridge the gap between the reward and the behavior. A token is anything that is a symbol of a later reinforcer; it is traded in for later rewards. Tokens can be poker chips, stickers, stars, buttons, or points, for example. A coin or dollar bill is a common example of a token-- the piece of paper itself is practically worthless, but the dollar is later traded in for other reinforcers. It is recommended that many chronic pain sufferers engage in regular relaxation exercises to decrease pain-contributing muscle tension. Often, many pain patients feel that they do not have the time to engage in recommended exercises. In this case, it may be helpful to design a plan in which points are earned for each time an exercise is completed. When a certain number of points are earned, the individual can go out to dinner or engage in some other desired activity.

Imagined (covert) reinforcers. The concept is to vividly imagine rewards contingent upon behavior. For example, once you finish an exercise routine, imagine yourself slim and trim lying on the beach in your new bathing suit.

Verbal Self-Reinforcement. The key is to praise yourself each time you perform your desired behavior. It is easy to see how someone may begin to feel depressed if they continually tell themselves negative things. This technique does exactly the opposite and can be an equally powerful technique. Praising yourself for a job well done can enhance your sense of self-efficacy and help keep up your motivation to continue the behavior change program.

Part Three

Specific Interventions for

Feelings, Thoughts, and Actions

Chapter 7

Visualization and Imagery

Background

Visualization and imagery exercises are soothing and pleasant activities that can enhance the depth of relaxation that you achieve through the progressive muscle relaxation exercises you learned in Chapter 4. One of the most popular applications of visualization techniques has been as an aid in preparing for and improving athletic performance as well as enhancing other types of performance skills (such as acting, playing a musical instrument, etc). Visualization techniques have also proved useful in helping people cope with chronic pain conditions. In this chapter we will cover each of these uses of visualization.

Visualization to Enhance Relaxation

Visualization can be a powerful aid for enhancing relaxation. We highly recommend that you learn the progressive muscle relaxation training (PRT) exercises discussed in Chapter 4 before adding visualization to your repertoire of stress management techniques. Our recommendation is based on the observation that people who are stressed and want to learn to relax, initially have a hard time pushing unwanted thoughts from their mind. Often people are thinking about the things that stress them, such as what they have to do later that day or about some unpleasant event that happened recently, and these thoughts keep their tension level high and make it difficult to implement a purely mental relaxation technique such as visualization. The advantage of learning PRT first is that the physical sensations of tensing and releasing the muscles provide a point of attentional focus, therefore making it easier for a person to develop the ability to push aside unwanted extraneous thoughts.

Developing Relaxing Imagery

You may have already begun to develop relaxing imagery while learning the progressive muscle relaxation exercises from chapter four. As you become relaxed during progressive muscle relaxation exercises it is not uncommon to have mental images of relaxing scenes such as lying on the beach, watching a beautiful sunset, or even floating on clouds. In this section we want to develop and sharpen your relaxing imagery. Start by following the three imagery building steps described in the box below and continuing on the top of the next page.

Developing Relaxing Imagery

1. Begin with the progressive muscle relaxation exercises from chapter four. Let your attention focus on the sensations of tension and relaxation as you proceed through the nine muscle groups. If worrisome or unwanted thoughts enter your mind, gently push them aside by returning your attention to the sensations you are creating in your muscles.

Developing Relaxing Imagery (continued)

2.   When you have gone through the PRT exercise remain in the relaxed state and breath very deeply and very slowly while you focus on what the sensation of relaxation feels like. It might feel light or heavy, warm or cool, bright or dark. These are just a few examples of how people commonly describe the sensation of relaxation. Just make a few mental notes as to the adjectives that best describe what the sensation of relaxation feels like to you.

3.   Now elaborate on the basic sensations that describe what relaxation feels like to you, and try to develop clear images that you can associate with the sensation of relaxation. For example, if relaxation feels very heavy, cool, and dark you might embellish these feelings by imagining yourself lying in the middle of a big bed where you sink deeply into the mattress which completely cushions and supports you. You might imagine looking up from the bed at a beautiful starry night as a pleasant cooling breeze gently rustles the leaves outside your open window. If you find that the sensation of relaxation feels more on the light, warm and bright end of the continuum you might imagine lying on the beach on a bright sunny day. The sensations of warmth and heaviness can be enhanced by imagining yourself sinking into the warm soft sand as you listen to the waves beating against the shore and the sea birds chirping in the distance. Feel the gentle ocean breeze as you inhale the distinctive smells of the ocean. You get to control the imagery in order to make it as pleasant as possible. Tailor the images to scenes that are especially relaxing for you.

This is your imagination at work, the imagery you create does not have to "make sense" in the real world. You can have a bed outside in the woods or on the beach. You can dictate that there will be no mosquitoes, that the sun is never too hot, that you are always perfectly safe. There are no rules; you own these images. Your only goal is to create vivid images that use all the sensory modalities (sight, sound, smell, taste, touch) that enhance relaxation for you. Your main purpose is to develop clear images and associate them with relaxing feelings so that you can use these images to induce relaxation in situations where other relaxation techniques might not be appropriate.

Letting Go With Visualization

Visualization can also be used to simply enhance the depth and the pleasure of the relaxation itself. For example some people find that the sensation of relaxation feels very light, as if they were floating. It is relatively easy to develop imagery where sensations of floating can be transformed into sensations of flying, and for many people (including SEG), the sensation of flight is very pleasant, relaxing and refreshing. As you finish the PRT exercise from chapter four continue to breath deeply and slowly and notice the sensation of lightness in your limbs and body. For your first flight let yourself float up out of the chair in a sitting position and then let your body gently return to the chair. Practice this imagery until you can "take-off" and "land" easily. Remember we are practicing imagery here. If you want to fly you cannot take your physics text with you. You can control your flight any way you want but a simple device is to lift your head up when you want to go up and down when you want to go down. Increase and decrease your speed with hands and arms (outstretched arms and spread fingers slow you down whereas arms flat against your side can speed you up) as well as legs and feet. Its fun to fly with the birds and skim over the clouds. Whether you want to fly or develop your own private relaxation world you need only practice the relaxation exercises in Chapter 4 and then use your imagination (and practice) developing vivid imagery to create your own relaxing environment.

Visualization to Prepare for Athletic Performance

Many trainers, coaches and sports psychologists advocate the use of visualization and mental imagery to enhance athletic performance. The idea is that you can have a "mini-workout" using mental rehearsal that will improve your skills and carry over to real competition the same way that physical practice does. Mental imagery works because your muscles react to imagined movement in the same way they do actual movements. Everything you have learned about imagery so far also applies to athletic performance. You must first be able to relax (Chapter 4) and you must realize that visualization is a skill that you will need to practice. Most people's visualization skills improve as a function of practice, even those people who initially have trouble forming clear images. Relaxation and practice are the two keys to successful visualization. These skills will help improve performance and, by making you feel better prepared, decrease performance anxiety. We have a separate chapter on controlling performance anxiety per se so don't practice these skills as if preparing for the day of a big competition (Chapter 10 has useful techniques for that). Use the skills in this section to prepare for any other practice day. You are just visualizing to correct problems and improve specific skills.

We are fortunate to have as a colleague Dr. Steven Danish, a well known sports psychologist and researcher who has worked with athletes from high school to the pros across a variety of different sports. He has shared with us some of the specific visualization techniques he uses with athletes to help them improve their performance. For athletic performance enhancement you will want to use both external and internal imagery.

External and Internal Imagery

Most of us have experience with external imagery. This refers to the visual perspective experienced as if you were watching your body perform a skill (as if you were watching yourself on a home movie). External imagery is recommended when you are first learning a new skill. External images can help you correct mistakes by allowing you to "see" the skill performed and identify the error. You then proceed to visually imagine correcting the flaw until it is mentally perfect. Internal imagery may take more practice but is the most crucial skill to work on. With internal imagery the visual perspective is through your own eyes. In contrast to external imagery, in which you are looking at your body as a spectator would, in internal imagery you are looking out of your own eyes and feeling the sensations of your body as you practice your athletic skill.

Assessing Your External and Internal Imagery Ability

Close your eyes and imagine yourself lying on your stomach on a beautiful ocean beach or anywhere else that is comfortable and relaxing for you. See yourself as if you were watching a home movie of yourself. If you can see the back of your head and the clothes on your back then you are able to use external imagery. To assess your internal imagery open your eyes and place your hand, palm towards your face, in front of your eyes. Wiggle your fingers in front of your face and notice what it looks like and <u>what it feels like</u>. Now put your hand down by your side, close your eyes and <u>imagine</u> your hand in front of your face and <u>imagine</u> wiggling your fingers. If you can see the palm of your hand and feel your fingers wiggling, then you are able to use internal imagery. With these disinctions in mind you are ready to practice mental imagery to improve your athletic performance.

Practicing Mental Imagery to Improve Athletic Performance

1. Relax your body using the progressive muscle relaxation techniques from Chapter 4. As you let all the tension out of the final muscle group continue to breathe very deeply and very slowly and notice what the sensation of relaxation feels like.

2. At the point of total relaxation begin to practice imagery by picturing an orange in front of you. Become aware of all aspects of the orange, its color, texture and smell. Peel the orange and remove a section and bite into it noticing what it tastes like. Put the section back in the orange and "rewind" your imagery so that you see the whole orange appear back in its original unpeeled form.

3. You are ready to practice visualizing your particular athletic event. Our example involves swimming. Use this example to create your own imagery for whatever sport you want to improve.

4. Study the arena, court, practice field, etc., where you routinely practice as if you were a spectator (external imagery). Study this place with the same intensity as you studied the orange, noticing as many of the sensory dimensions as you can. Imagine you are a swimmer observing the outdoor practice pool. The water is clear and cool. You can see the light blue bottom of the pool giving the water the appearance of being blue as well. There is a faint smell of chlorine, the sun feels warm.

5. Erase these images and return your focus to the sensations of relaxation. Imagine yourself leisurely warming up for your event. Decide which area of your game you want to work on in this visualization session. As a swimmer you will be working on the freestyle turn. After a few leisurely laps in the pool picture yourself doing freestyle turns, watching yourself as if you were a spectator watching another swimmer. Try to notice as much as possible about how you execute the flip turn; look at your body in relation to the wall and the water. Obtain a clear picture of how you execute these movements.

Practicing Mental Imagery to Improve Athletic Performance
(Continued)

6. Imagine a model who is exceptionally proficient at performing the same skill you are trying to improve. Watch the model perform the movements in slow motion, taking note of each aspect of the performance. Our swimmer imagines Janet Evans doing free style turns. Carefully observe the details of the turn technique; the strong last stroke, the legs flipping over partially tucked as they move through the water, the push off from the side of the pool, streamlined, with a strong pull from the deep arm as the head pops to the surface.

7. Imagine yourself and the model performing the same skill on a split screen television. You are both performing in slow motion. Notice how your performance differs from that of the model. Choose several aspects of the model's performance that is better than yours and see clearly what you must do to improve your turn (or free throw, stride, serve, swing, etc.)

8. Now make the transition from external to internal imagery. Let the model disappear and visualize yourself actually performing the movements. You are in your own body, taking the perspective from your own eyes as you perform rather than as a spectator watching yourself. Now you will <u>feel</u> yourself performing the motor movements. My swimmer no longer watches herself as a spectator. She sees the wall of the pool as she swims towards it. You see the wall as you approach it, feel the strength of your last pull, see how your legs come over and make contact with the wall and then feel the speed and strength of the push-off from the wall. Feel where your back and legs are, you should not be able to see them. Focus on those aspects of your performance that you identified as areas that you need to work on.

Steps 2 through 8 should only take about five minutes once you become familiar with the exercise. Practice your selected skill until you find yourself consistently performing correctly. When you feel comfortable and confident open your eyes and you should feel relaxed and eager for physical practice. The results of practicing imagery may seem almost magical at times but its benefits are not due to magic or hocus pocus. Imagined practice can have the same benefits as physical practice. You must practice visualization skills to become proficient at them and achieve the greatest benefits. If you have trouble with the imagery exercises there is a section at the end of this chapter on overcoming roadblocks that might help you.

Health Related Applications of Visualization

Many proponents of imagery training suggest that visualization techniques facilitate communication between mind and body to enhance the healing process. For example visualization has been advocated as a way to help cancer and AIDS patients increase the integrity of their immune system. Basically the idea is to visualize the healthy lymphocytes of the immune system attacking and destroying the cancerous or virus ridden cells. While many studies have shown that imagery is an effective attention diverting technique and relaxation enhancer, well controlled studies demonstrating that it promotes healing per se are lacking at this time. On the other hand, visualization can certainly do no harm and it is possible that visualization may promote the type of direct healing that its advocates suggest. Visualization can enhance relaxation and may promote a sense of control and active participation in one's own health care that serves as a valuable adjunct to sound medical intervention.

Visualization to Cope with Chronic Pain

Visualization techniques can be a powerful tool to help a person cope better with a chronic pain condition. In Chapter 16 we discuss stress management techniques that have been demonstrated to be effective in reducing the frequency and intensity of pain episodes among persons suffering from head and facial pain. Chapter 16 covers stress management techniques that have been shown to have a direct effect on the pain itself, and which bring substantial relief to the pain sufferer. However, there is no magic bullet to eliminate all pain and therefore psychologists have looked for strategies to help people cope with whatever residual pain remains after other stress management techniques have been used. Visualization techniques have proved useful for helping pain patients cope better with daytime pain by providing a distraction from the pain and allowing the person to "wall off" or otherwise isolate the pain. Moreover, since chronic pain can be particularly debilitating by disrupting the quality of nighttime sleep, visualization has been applied to help facilitate sound sleep for the chronic pain patient.

Numerous studies have demonstrated that when people focus their attention on their pain, they report much higher levels of pain intensity and unpleasantness than when they are distracted with another task. In the daytime it is relatively easy to distract oneself or to "take your mind off" the pain. However, when pain intensity is very high (a seven or above on a ten point scale) and is constantly present day after day it is often hard to focus on anything other than the pain. Unlike the skills presented in Chapter 16 which are designed to actually decrease the intensity of pain, visualization will not change the intensity of the pain but will allow a person to compartmentalize the pain so that it does not completely occupy your attention.

Imagery is useful in this context because it diverts attention from something unpleasant (pain) to an image of something pleasant (pain melting like ice). Often people find this much more difficult at night when there is nothing to do except to try to fall asleep. At night when the lights are off and it gets fairly quiet the only stimuli to attend to are those created inside your own body. When the stimuli your body creates are painful they are hard to ignore unless you consciously try to override them with images you create in your own mind. The steps below will help you build your imagery skills to create pain relief for either daytime or nighttime purposes.

Imagery for Pain Relief

1. Relax

Relax deeply using the progressive muscle relaxation (PRT) exercises described in Chapter 4. Go through the visualization exercises described in the first section of this chapter to enhance your state of relaxation through visualization. Develop relaxing imagery that fits the sensations of relaxation that you experience.

Imagery for Pain Relief (continued)

2. Imagine your pain.

Once you are proficient at the relaxation and general visualization exercises think of an image that represents the particular type, quality, and intensity of your pain.

Some examples are pins and needles sticking in the flesh at the site of pain site, a searing sun at the point of pain, a hammer pounding, or vise turning at site of pain. What's important here is for you to make the image of your pain personally relevant.

3. Imagine your pain relief.

Change the image of your pain to something pleasant, or at least tolerable. Visualize a therapeutic image or process which represents the release of pain.

Examples of how the pain images presented in #2 might be transformed could be snowflakes lying lightly on the skin instead of pins and needles in the flesh, a cooling moon emitting a soothing, cooling reflection of the sun, a hammer fading or dissolving away or the vice retracting, slowly disintegrating.

Remember, conjure up these images while you are in a relaxed state. You do not have to force the images to appear. When you are relaxed, images will come to you. Select the images that are personally relevant to you and that best depict your pain and its release.

Other images that many chronic pain patients find beneficial allow you to isolate your pain to a particular place. The pain is still there, but it is more manageable because it is more localized. For example, imagine putting the pain in a box and locking it up. Or using the pain to blow up a balloon and then releasing the balloon. The idea is to transform the mental image of the pain into a mental image that allows the pain to be more manageable. Experiment. You have nothing to lose but the pain.

4. Imagine the positive benefits.

Visualize yourself feeling better, smiling and laughing, moving around freely, enjoying the people and things around you. Create an image of yourself which is active and positive and in good health. Some people report success here with using the techniques described in the section on visualization to enhance athletic performance.

Overcoming Roadblocks

The roadblocks to successful application of imagery techniques are very similar to those described in Chapter 4 for relaxation training. If you did not learn the relaxation techniques in Chapter 4 because you did not have enough time to practice you will not be able to add the visualization techniques to your repertoire of relaxation skills. For some people however, reading about the visualization sparks their interest in relaxation techniques in general and increases motivation to find the time to practice these skills. Go back to the end of Chapter 4 to see how little time is really required to learn relaxation skills.

A very different roadblock sometimes occurs for some people who are highly motivated, practice diligently, but just can not seem to develop vivid images. If this describes you, chances are you are trying too hard. You need to be relaxed to let the images come to you. Do not try to force the images. When you first learn to ride a bike there is that definitive moment when everybody lets go and you have to find your balance for yourself. If you are too tense you will fall. You need to be able to relax to find your balance and in the same manner find the imagery that enhances your relaxation. Have you ever tried to find the hidden 3-D image in the colorful Magic Eye books and posters that have been so popular for several years? The 3-D image pops out at you when you relax and stare at the picture hypnotically. The same strategy applies to visualization.

Finally, for some people visualization is difficult because it does not seem scientific enough. That is, while progressive muscle relaxation training in Chapter 4 has a clear physiological basis and a great deal of research to support its efficacy, visualization may seem too hokey, or too much like hocus pocus to take seriously. If you find yourself with these types of reservations about the technique then concentrate your energies on the progressive muscle relaxation techniques. PRT is the most essential of the emotion focused techniques and will serve you well in any situation that calls for emotion focused coping. Consider the wise words of Daniel Dennett, author of Consciousness Explained (which has little to do with visualization per se but is full of insightful observations). Dennett notes that the "absence of representation is not equivalent to the representation of absence." In other words, just because you cannot imagine or visualize something does not mean that others cannot. Nor does your current failure in visualization preclude you from using the technique with success in the future. My brother stared at those 3-D art posters for years and never saw a thing until one day the picture just "popped out of the page" in front of him. If visualization seems like work don't practice it for now. Learn some of the other techniques and come back to visualization another time.

Tracking Your Progress

Whether you use visualization simply to enhance relaxation or to help improve athletic performance or cope with pain, you will make better progress if you keep a practice sheet. We recommend that you keep a very simple record sheet where you note when you practice, how long you practice, and importantly the quality of your imagery. Once you get the knack of visualization you will not need to keep a record sheet if you are using visualization as a relaxation enhancer. You will just be able to do it whenever you want. The record sheet is most important when you are just getting started to give you hard data on how much you have actually practiced and to see your progress. You should try to practice the visualization 3-4 times a week for one or two five minute sessions. If you are practicing to improve athletic competence you may want to practice more frequently and you will need to keep a practice log throughout your training to track your progress with each of the specific athletic skills you are working on. The section on Tracking your Progress from Chapter 3 will help you tailor a record sheet for your particular goals.

Chapter 8
Controlling Anger and Building Frustration Tolerance
Rationale

Anger is a normal everyday emotion that, like anxiety, can lead to serious negative consequences for both our mental and physical health if left unresolved. Anger can be a response to stressful circumstances (someone cuts you off in traffic) as well as a cause of stress (feeling angry may lead to aggressive behavior and/or guilt). There is nothing wrong or bad about experiencing anger. When anger is dealt with in an appropriately assertive manner its negative effects are minimized and, in fact, can provide the spark for adaptive change. Anger becomes a problem for people when they either 1) hold it inside and let it eat away at them, never really resolving the negative emotion and/or 2) when anger leads to inappropriate aggressive behavior. Anger control problems refer to both the experience of excessive and unwanted angry <u>feelings</u> as well as aggressive/hurtful <u>behavior</u> that may accompany angry feelings. Interventions aimed at changing, thoughts, actions, and feelings from Chapter 6 can all be effective in managing anger. In this chapter we will emphasize techniques that will help you manage anger by lowering your level of emotional arousal via emotion-focused and cognitive techniques. Direct action techniques for changing aggressive behavior that arise from excessive anger are covered in a subsequent chapter on assertiveness (Chapter 11). In general, when anger levels are very high it is difficult to <u>act</u> effectively. Therefore, in this chapter we emphasize emotional regulation techniques designed to reduce the intensity of the angry feelings.

Deep Breathing

One of the simplest and most effective anger management techniques is to take three deep breaths and let the tension out of your shoulders when you feel your level of anger rising. Deep breathing as discussed in Chapter 2 is the most fundamental emotional regulation technique you can learn to combat excessive levels of anger (and other negative emotion). Review Chapter 2 now if it has been some time since you practiced this technique.

Positive Coping Statements

Positive coping statements can be extremely effective aids to anger control. Take the generic coping statements presented in the box on the next page and tailor them to your particular personality and situation. You can tailor these statements by substituting the names of real people and describing real situations. Put the statements in words that you are comfortable with (For example, the first generic coping statement "I'm not going to let this upset me" might become: "I'm not going to let this disagreement with my husband about where we are going on vacation upset me."). Repeat to yourself the positive coping statements you develop as you breathe deeply and slowly when angered. You might be concerned that using positive coping statements is tantamount to condoning the things which make you angry. This is not the case. Positive coping statements coupled with deep breathing is a technique that gives you control over your response to the situation. After you have better control over your anger you may want to use one of the action oriented techniques (e.g., assertiveness skills building to try to hange the situation in a constructive manner).

Developing Positive Coping Statements Tailored for Your Specific Situations

Generic Coping Statement   **Individually Tailored Statement**

I'm not going to let this upset me.   _____

                                                                _____

I'm going to keep my cool & stay in control.   _____

                                                                _____

I wish this were not happening to me but
I can handle it.   _____

                                                                _____

Getting upset will only make the situation worse.   _____

                                                                _____

I can accept this even if I do not agree with it.   _____

                                                                _____

I am stronger than this emotion.   _____

                                                                _____

I cannot control how this situation turns
out but I can control me.   _____

                                                                _____

I have a better chance of getting what
I want if I do not blow up over this.   _____

                                                                _____

He might ruin his day over this but
I'm not going to let him ruin mine.   _____

                                                                _____

Escape Valves for Anger

When deep breathing and positive coping statements do not bring your level of emotional arousal down and you are trying to resist the urge to act aggressively on your anger and frustration, find an escape valve.

Escape Valves for Anger

1. Leave the situation. This is a problem-focused strategy that puts distance between you and what is triggering your anger. This will give you a chance to cool down and use the breathing technique and positive coping statements more effectively. Just as importantly, leaving the situation will prevent you from acting impulsively or aggressively and possibly making the situation much worse.

2. Exercise the anger away. Walk, run, or do whatever other type of physical activity that best suits you in order to try to work off the pent up arousal. Exercise until you are tired and the angry feelings have subsided.

3. Isometrics. If your ability to leave the situation and exercise is limited (for example you may have kids to watch, or have limited mobility) try isometric exercises. Put your hands against the wall and push. Push hard. Push until your muscles are exhausted.

4. Yell and Scream. Literally. Yell and scream at the top of your lungs until you are exhausted. But yell and scream by yourself (for example in the bedroom or bathroom) not at somebody else.

5. Hit Your Pillow. If you are so angry you feel you have to hit something, go to the bedroom and beat the stuffing out of your pillow. Get a towel and flail away at the bed until you are exhausted.

Anger and Unrealistic Beliefs

For many people angry <u>feelings</u> and <u>behavior</u> are precipitated by unrealistic beliefs about the way the world and life "should" be. Many people get angry when they experience a discrepancy between how things are and how they think things "ought" to be. Maladaptive beliefs discussed in Chapter 5, such as "I must be perfect" or "everybody must like me" often precipitate anxiety. Beliefs such as "life must be fair," "others should treat me as well as I treat them," "I must get what I want and deserve" are all common "musts," "shoulds'" and "oughts" associated with angry feelings.

When life is not fair to us it is very difficult to look at our own thoughts and beliefs as contributors to the anger and frustration we feel. Yet the unvarnished truth is that life is not fair, never was, never will be. We set ourselves up to be perpetually angry and miserable people if the criteria for happiness is an ideal world where we are always treated fairly. Some would argue that if you eat a full dinner tonight and have a roof over your head you are better off than 70% of the world's population. Don't worry, be happy. Life's a beach. These phrases and truisms are small consolation however when *you* do the right thing, when *you* play by the rules, and others do not, yet others seem to profit more.

Yet if you allow yourself to stay angry because someone has done you wrong, letting anger fester like an open wound, you give up control over your own emotional and physical health. Do you want the people and institutions that treat you unfairly to have that kind of power over your physical and emotional well being? People and things do not have the power to *make* you angry unless you give the power of emotional regulation away. Go back to Chapter 5 and work on the exercises on refuting and changing maladaptive beliefs, because how you think very clearly influences how you feel. The idea that it is unrealistic to believe that life should always be fair is sometimes hard for people to swallow because they mistakenly think that accepting things as they are is equivalent to approving of the way things are. Accepting is not the same thing as approving.

Controlling Anger Through Forgiveness

One of our most distinguished colleagues, Dr. Everett Worthington, was recently awarded the VCU College of Humanities and Sciences Distinguished Teaching Award. His comments upon accepting this award speak volumes towards the power of forgiveness in resolving anger. Dr. Worthington suggests that in order to let go of anger by forgiving those who have wronged us, we must find a way to empathize with the other person. We must try to see the events from the other person's perspective. These are his words:

This past New Year's eve night, my mother was murdered in her home. Her death has affected me almost as much as any event ever has, and I am still a bit on the emotional surface.

When I received the call from my brother on New Year's morning, I was stunned. I tried to cope with it the way I try to cope with many unpleasant events in my life--through action. I rushed around getting ready to drive to Knoxville, throwing clothes in a suitcase and hustling furiously to and fro. It was only after I was packed and sitting at the table comforting my daughter that I broke down and simply cried.

Driving to Knoxville with my sister and her husband, I replayed many of the good times and bad with my mother.

That night, my brother, my sister, and I sat amid the seventeen loaves of bread, twenty pies, and five plates of cold cuts that neighbors and friends had provided out of their generosity. We began to talk about the details of the murder that were known to us because it was my brother who had walked in on my mother's body.

She had been beaten to death with a crowbar. Blood was everywhere--on the door, the walls, soaked through the carpet. The perpetrator had also completely trashed the house--breaking all mirrors and every reflecting surface in the house.

Rage bubbled up like lava. I found my self saying, "I'd like to have him alone in a room with a baseball bat for thirty minutes."

My sister said, "I'd just take ten minutes."

My brother added, "I'd take two hours."

We were furious.

That night at 3:00 am, I couldn't sleep. I sat awake in my bed as I tried, though the tears, to compose a eulogy to my mother, and I thought about forgiveness.

The irony is that I had, only days before, finished writing a book on forgiveness. In it, my co-authors (Mike McCullough and Steve Sandage) and I had argued that empathy was the key to forgiveness. Could I empathize with the youth who had done this terrible thing to my mother?

I imagined how her assailant might feel upon slipping into a house that he thought was deserted, only to be surprised by someone saying behind him, "What are you doing in here?"

He turned, lashed out and hit my mother three times with the crowbar he had used to break the window. He did a terrible thing. Nothing will change or minimize the evil of his act.

Yet, where he had lashed out in fear and surprise and anger, I had stood in the kitchen earlier and contemplated beating him to death with a baseball bat. When I saw the evil that I was capable of plotting, I was humbled. I was able to forgive him and let go of my desire to see him put to death for his crime. I, of course, think he should not be released to perpetrate a similar crime again, but my desire for retribution had evaporated and I have since felt at peace.

I learned a lot from that painful experience.

I learned first that empathy really is a key to forgiving those who have hurt us.

More than that, I learned a valuable lesson about my personal faith--that no matter how deep the pit, God is deeper still.........

Most of the day to day anger that we feel has far more petty origins than what set off the anger that bubbled up like lava in Dr. Worthington. Just reading his story may be enough inspiration to give up the more petty angers of the day. The belief in a supreme being is virtually universal across cultures. Prayer, confession, and forgiveness are powerful forces in the lives of many people that can be tapped in times of intense anger along with the breathing, imagery, and cognitive restructuring techniques presented here.

Tracking Your Progress

You should use a structured diary from Chapter 3 to figure out the ABCs of your anger control problem and develop a recording system that works well for you. You will probably want to record both the frequency of your angry episodes as well as the intensity of your anger. Again, Chapter 3 provides good examples of how to keep both of these types of records.

Overcoming Roadblocks

Unlike many of the other stress management techniques described so far, lack of time is usually not a major roadblock in learning to control anger and build frustration tolerance. A person who is motivated to change can learn these emotional regulation techniques without taking a lot of time. However, it is still a big commitment in terms of effort. If you are committed to learning to better manage your anger we recommend that you return to Chapter 6 and review some of the general techniques presented there that may help you with your specific type of anger problem. In particular, many people learning to better control their anger benefit from the techniques aimed at Modifying Old Antecedents and Arranging New Antecedents. Look through this section again to find techniques that you can tailor to your own situation.

Chapter 9

Stopping Unwanted Thoughts

Background

Thought stopping and limited worry techniques are cognitive stress management interventions that help a person eliminate unwanted, intrusive, usually repetitive types of thinking. In the past thought stopping has been cited as a treatment for obsessive and phobic thinking. Full fledged obsessions are experienced as intrusive thoughts that the person experiences as uncontrollable and anxiety provoking. Very frequently, but not always, obsessive thinking is associated with compulsive behaviors. A person may worry excessively about germs and acquiring some disease from germs and feel compelled to wash their hands dozens of times a day in order to manage their anxiety. Anxiety diminishes temporarily but the obsessional thoughts return and the person feels the urge to wash their hands again and again. Other frequently occurring obsessive/compulsive patterns center around worrisome thoughts about doors or windows left unlocked or appliances (stoves, irons, coffeepots, etc.) left on, and these thoughts are followed by compulsive checking rituals. A person may spend literally hours repeatedly checking to make sure everything is turned off before leaving the house. Obsessive/compulsive behavior in its extreme forms is a serious condition for which thought stopping alone will not likely be an effective intervention. Similarly, the intrusive thoughts and flashbacks often experienced by trauma victims (e.g., people who suffer from post-traumatic stress disorder) are usually not amenable to thought stopping and limited worry procedures. Treatment of both of these types of intrusive thinking problems are better corrected with one of the exposure techniques discussed in our text book. We recommend the implementation of these techniques for these particular problems be carried out with the aid of a cognitive-behavior therapist.

There are many other forms of unwanted thinking that the procedures in this chapter have proved effective in reducing or eliminating. In general, repetitive worrisome thinking that has not yet taken on a truly obsessive quality can be managed with thought stopping techniques. Another type of unwanted thinking that thought stopping is effective in combating is repetitive daydreams. For some people, repetitive daydreams emerge in an intrusive fashion fostering procrastination and inaction in situations where direct action would be a more effective coping strategy.

Thought Stopping Rationale

Thought stopping was briefly introduced in Chapter 6 as one of several antecedent based techniques that foster the development of situational triggers for adaptive coping skills that you are trying to build. The thought stopping technique requires you to actively engage in your worrisome or troubling thinking and then abruptly terminate the thinking with a fairly dramatic aversive stimulus. Typical thought interrupting stimuli include shouting the word "STOP" while you stand up or pound the table or engage in some other dramatic motor movement. Some authors suggest the use of a rubber band on the wrist which is snapped at the same time the word "STOP" is shouted.

The learning principles which presumably account for successful thought stopping are threefold. First, the thought interrupting stimulus is distracting and the imperative self instruction to STOP is incompatible with continuing the unwanted thinking. Second, once distracted from the unwanted thoughts the person is in a position to substitute more adaptive coping statements that are incompatible with the unwanted thoughts. Both of these learning mechanisms explain why thought stopping can be a useful adjunct to other interventions that involve changing situational influences on your behavior. Sometimes, however, the main goal is to simply stop unwanted thoughts. The learning principle at work in this case is simple punishment. The thought interrupting stimulus is aversive and punishing, therefore reducing the frequency of the behavior which precedes it (the unwanted thoughts).

Thought Stopping Procedures

1. Lose Your Inhibitions
Practice in a place where you will not feel overly concerned about shouting out loud.

2. Create the Unwanted Thoughts
Allow yourself to produce the unwanted thoughts. Thought stopping works best if you actually let the unwanted thoughts occur rather than imagining the situation that the thoughts occur in. If you are bothered by intrusive thoughts about germs think about all the germs that you have come in contact with today. If you tend to worry about whether you turned off the oven (or iron or...) consider the possibility that you forgot to turn it off today. If you have a repetitive unwanted fantasy let yourself get immersed in the fantasy. Whatever your usual worrisome or problematic thought is, you can usually let it emerge just by letting yourself think about it.

3. Interrupt the Unwanted Thoughts
Interrupt the unwanted thoughts by standing up and loudly shouting "STOP." You actually have to shout "STOP." If the interruption is not dramatic the technique will not work. Think about neutral non anxious thoughts for 30 seconds while you remain standing. If the unwanted thoughts return in thirty seconds (they probably will not) shout "STOP" again.

4. Gradually Fade the Shouted Interruption
When you can eliminate the unwanted thought for 30 seconds or more by shouting "STOP," you will begin to fade out the shouting and replace the thought interrupting stimulus with gradually less vocal cues. Move from shouting "STOP" to simply saying "STOP" in a normal voice. Then move to a whispered "STOP." Finally shout "STOP" to yourself subvocally. Hear yourself say "STOP" in your head by tightening your vocal cords and move your tongue as if you were saying it out loud but only say it to yourself.

5. Substitute More Adaptive Thoughts
Once you have progressed to the point where you can stop the unwanted thoughts by saying "STOP" to yourself begin substituting more adaptive coping statements in place of the unwanted thoughts.

Overcoming Roadblocks

Although thought stopping is an extremely simple and straightforward technique there are several potential problems with successful application of this procedure.

1. The first problem many people have with thought stopping is that they are very inhibited about shouting the word "STOP." They feel foolish and worry that others will hear them. If this describes you and these feeling of foolishness prevent you from trying this technique then return to Chapter 5 (changing unrealistic thoughts and beliefs) to learn to dispute and counter your overconcern about what others think of you. You do not want to let rigid beliefs about how you "should" behave, or unrealistic concerns about what others think of you, prevent you from implementing a technique that has proved quite effective in reducing or eliminating unwanted thoughts of mild to moderate severity.

2. Sometimes people have difficulty creating the unwanted thoughts "on demand" for several reasons. Most frequently, it is because the situations that elicit the unwanted thoughts occur very infrequently making it difficult to realistically create the thoughts.

For example, a woman who described herself as slightly anxious about flying had very troubling thoughts about her child being sucked out of the airplane and into the engines while in flight. These thoughts tormented her tremendously while in flight (whether her child was flying with her or not) and she would arrive at her destination completely drained. The woman knew that these thoughts were absurd and she was not troubled by them at all when not flying (she might think about them while reflecting on how stressful flying was but she could stop them at any time). But in flight the thoughts were very intrusive and anxiety provoking. In this situation, she could not inhibit them and at times during the flight the prospect of her child being ripped from her arms and sucked into the engines seemed like a very real possibility. Even if she were a truly frequent flyer thought stopping as described above would have been difficult because in a situation where you are surrounded by others it is not a maladaptive belief to think that it would be inappropriate to stand up and shout "STOP."

In situations like this thought stopping begins by producing the unwanted thoughts in the imagination. The woman was instructed first in relaxation training (Chapter 4) and then received some basic instruction in visualization (Chapter 7) in order to learn to vividly imagine being on the airplane from an internal perspective. Then she was able to freely produce the unwanted thoughts engendered by the flight situation. From there she was able to implement the thought stopping as described in steps 3-5 above.

Basically the recommendation we make is that if you can produce the unwanted thoughts "in vivo" (in real life situations) and can implement the thought interruption in that situation you should do so. If you cannot, then use the visualization techniques in Chapter 7 to visualize the situation that produces the unwanted thoughts and then implement the thought interruption stimulus (stand-up and shout "STOP").

3. It is possible that you will be able to readily put yourself in the situation that produces the

unwanted thoughts but not be able to use the verbal thought interruption stimulus. For example, on crowded elevators you are consumed by thoughts that everyone is staring at you. You cannot get these thoughts out of your mind but you do not want shout "STOP" in the elevator. You might choose to create the unwanted thoughts through visualization as suggested in item two just above. Or you may want to try thought interruption while in the real life situation (e.g., on the elevator) but use a painful stimulus for thought interruption as you shout the word "STOP" to yourself subvocally. You may snap a rubber band on your wrist or dig your finger nails into your palms as the painful stimulus. This is not our first choice of techniques, but if you choose to try this version of the technique remember the thought interruption must be dramatic and abrupt.

Limited Worry Rationale

In a limited worry intervention the goal is to establish designated periods of worry time where a person thinks and worries intensively about his or her concerns. Worrying is not permitted during other periods of the day. The rationale for this approach is that by isolating the worry process to a restricted set of circumstances the person is limiting the number of cues associated with the worrisome thoughts. This is a version of the technique described in Chapter 6 concerning narrowing antecedent control. The idea is to change the circumstances and therefore, the triggers of the worrisome behavior.

Limited Worry Procedures

1. Use a structured diary from Chapter 3 to closely observe your thinking during the day. Identify the situations and consequences that surround episodes of worry. Pay particular attention to what triggers your worry.

2. Establish a half hour worry period to take place at the same time and in the same place every day.

3. Do not permit any worrying outside of your designated worry period. When you catch yourself worrying and ruminating, put it off until your worry period.

4. When worrisome thoughts intrude outside of your worry period divert your attention away from these thoughts by focusing your attention on the task at hand or anything else in your immediate environment. Some people choose to use the thought stopping technique described above at this stage if they are unable to distract themselves from the worrisome thought.

5. Importantly, you must actually use your worry period to worry. Spend a half an hour intensively thinking and worrying about your concerns. By enforcing this practice worry period you help break the chain of cues which trigger your worry during the rest of the day.

More recently Barlow and colleagues have developed a worry exposure treatment to eliminate unwanted worrisome thoughts in patients suffering from Generalized Anxiety Disorder. Research testing the effectiveness of this intervention has been very favorable. You might consider professional help if your unwanted thoughts interfere with the quality of your life but you find yourself unable to use the techniques presented here to eliminate your troublesome thinking.

Chapter 10

Stress Inoculation Training

Rationale

Stress inoculation training (SIT) is a planful cognitive coping strategy. SIT is not a single technique but a unique combination of techniques including most of the techniques already covered in this workbook. This chapter provides you with a chance to put together a stress management program for yourself using as many of the previous techniques as you want. The combination of techniques presented here is designed to help you develop general coping skills for resolving and coping with specific immediate and future stressors. Donald Meichenbaum developed stress inoculation training and his work has been adapted by others for use with a variety of different types of stress-related problems. The self-management form of stress inoculation presented here is adapted from Meichenbaum's (1985) work.

The focus of SIT is in the cognitive domain of functioning but it includes emotional regulation and direct action techniques as well. SIT emphasizes the fact that how you interpret and appraise a situation influences your emotional and behavioral reactions to stressors while also acknowledging that thoughts, emotions, physiological reactions, and behavior are all interrelated. The cognitive coping techniques utilized by SIT (some you are already familiar with while others will be new) are supplemented by other types of interventions to complement the effectiveness of the cognitive techniques. One of the advantages of SIT is that it fosters a sense of self-efficacy, increasing your confidence in your ability to control your reactions to, and ability to cope with, the stressors in your life. Indeed, the term stress inoculation suggests that new coping skills will act as "psychological antibodies" to protect you from the adverse effects of stress in the future. Note that the object of SIT is not to eliminate stress completely, but to use stress as a signal, an opportunity to problem solve and learn and apply new skills.

STRESS INOCULATION TRAINING PROCEDURES

There are three phases in self-directed Stress Inoculation Training, the Self Assessment and Problem Conceptualization Phase, Skills Acquisition and Rehearsal Phase, and the Application and Follow Through Phase. Several of the techniques included in SIT have been presented in earlier chapters of this workbook. We recommend that you first review this chapter in its entirety to get an overview of how the various techniques are interrelated in SIT. After you have read this chapter decide which of the previous chapters you want to review before actually implementing SIT.

CONCEPTUALIZATION PHASE

Self assessment is the key to identifying and defining the stress-related problems you want to address with stress inoculation procedures. Chapter 3 in this workbook reviews the self assessment procedures that you will need to carry out in order to conceptualize your stress-related problems in terms that will allow the successful application of SIT. By keeping a stress log in the form of a structured diary you will be able to describe your problems as behaviors (thoughts, feelings,& actions) in a situation. You will be able to see that your stress reactions are generally tied to specific situations and you will be able to identify the thoughts that you have that accelerate your stress response. You will and use the data you collect on yourself to identify targets for intervention with SIT.

SKILLS ACQUISITION AND REHEARSAL PHASE

Stress inoculation training provides a chance to develop a tailored treatment package that integrates many of the techniques covered in previous chapters.

1. Relaxation Training

Even though stress inoculation focuses primarily on cognitive interventions, deep breathing and relaxation training are essential skills that SIT draws on. Therefore you need to be proficient at relaxation for SIT to be an effective stress management intervention for you. Chapters 2 and 4 cover deep breathing ☺ and progressive muscle relaxation training (PRT). In this chapter we introduce a shorter version of PRT that you will use with new visualization exercises presented at the end of the chapter. It is important for you to be familiar with the full length relaxation exercise presented in Chapter 4 before you proceed with the relaxation exercises described in this chapter.

2. Cognitive Strategies

Stress inoculation training draws on several of the cognitive interventions already described in the workbook and introduces several others.

Refuting Irrational Beliefs. Changing unrealistic thoughts and beliefs is a building block skill presented in Chapter 5. The fundamental cognitive technique in stress inoculation is developing an appreciation for how unrealistic and rigid expectations about ourselves and others create stress. Learning how we appraise and interpret events in our lives is the key first step to managing stress in the SIT approach. Expecting to be liked by everyone, having unreachable standards ("I must be perfect"), expecting life to be fair all the time, are all examples of stress inducing beliefs. These beliefs influence how we evaluate and interpret life events. When we hold ourselves and others to unrealistically high standards we overreact to minor daily hassles and often experience tension and distress.

Self-Instructional Training (Guided Self-Dialogue). Stress coping thoughts are positive coping statements that you develop and tailor to a specific stressful encounter that help guide you through the stressful encounter. In Chapter 9 (Controlling Anger) positive coping statements for use when confronting and handling the stressor were introduced. You can actually think of a stressful encounter as having at least three different phases. For each phase you develop positive coping statements to help you through that phase of the encounter. The three types of statements and examples of each are provided below. Your task is to reformulate these statements (and create others) that will apply to your own specific stressful situations.

1. **Preparing for the Stressor**. Use preparatory statements to focus on planning and preparing for the stressor and combating negative thinking.

> ### Generic Coping Statements
> What do I have to do?
> I can work out a plan and handle this.
> What are some helpful things I can do instead of worrying?
> Feeling anxious is normal; I'll take three deep breaths.
> If I get ready for this I won't feel as anxious.
> Stop worrying and start preparing.

2. **Confronting and Handling the Stressor**. During the actual stressful encounter have positive coping statements prepared that will help you manage your stress by controlling the stress response itself, remain focused on the task, and reassure yourself that you can handle the situation.

> ### Generic Coping Statements
> Tension is my cue to take three deep breaths and exhale the tension away.
> This is not so big a deal that I can't handle it.
> One step at a time.
> I can convince myself to do it.
> Focus on handling <u>this</u> situation that I'm in <u>now</u>; one situation at a time.
> Don't catastrophize.

3. **Evaluation of Coping Efforts and Self-Rewards**. After the stressful encounter evaluate the effectiveness of your coping strategies and make a point to use self praise to reward coping attempts. Do not expect perfection from yourself. Change can be sudden but more often successful coping comes gradually with practice.

> ### Generic Coping Statements
> That wasn't as bad as I made it out to be.
> I feel more in control each time I use this procedure.
> What can I learn from my coping attempts in that situation.
> I handled that situation pretty well.
> I did well and next time I'll do even better.
> I can congratulate myself just for trying.

APPLICATION AND FOLLOW THROUGH PHASE

1. Imagery Rehearsal Overview.

Imagery rehearsal is a technique that allows you to rehearse in your imagination the adaptive coping responses developed in the skills acquisition phase of training, before trying the new skills out in real life. The type of imagery you will use is similar to the visualization exercises described in Chapter 7. To practice imagery rehearsal you will first need to develop a stressful event hierarchy and be able to generate positive coping statements for each of the stressful situations that you identify. Then you will use the relaxation exercise described below to become relaxed and then visualize yourself in each of the stressful situations. While visualizing yourself in the stressful situation you will imagine yourself actually using the positive coping statements and feeling more in control of your stress level. Now that you have a general overview of imagery rehearsal let's go over the specifics of how it works.

2. Stressful Event Hierarchy: Guidelines and Example

An example of a stressful event hierarchy is presented on the following page. The person in the example is a full time college student who also happens to be a single mother who works almost full time (30 hrs/week). This student successfully used stress-inoculation procedures to learn to better manage the stress she experienced from trying to juggle her multiple roles and their demands in her life. Guidelines for creating a stressful events hierarchy are outlined in the box below:

Guidelines for Creating a Stressful Events Hierarchy

1. The hierarchy is a list of about 20 stressful life situations that are currently occurring or that are highly likely to occur in the future. Use your self-monitoring data and stress diary from the self assessment phase to develop your list of stressful situations.

2. Your list of stressful situations should range from mildly anxiety provoking (SUDs of 5) to extremely anxiety provoking (SUDs of 100) with about five point increments between stressful events.

3. Stressful life situations should represent various areas of your life (i.e. family, occupation, friends, finances, etc).

4. Description of the stressful events are brief but should easily elicit a vivid image of the scene. The descriptions in the example hierarchy are a "thumbnail" sketch of the problem. Make sure you can develop specific descriptions and vivid imagery for each item.

STRESSFUL EVENT HIERARCHY EXAMPLE

Rank	Stressful Event	SUDs
1	Planning for Christmas holiday	5
2	Rush to get to 8:00 A.M. class on time	10
3	Computer lab assignment	15
4	Shopping for best friend's wedding	20
5	House cleaning	25
6	Catching up on Saturday with housework and bills	30
7	Finding a reliable sitter for son	35
8	Disagreement with ex-husband over child support	40
9	Oral presentation in class	45
10	Writing papers for school	50
11	Shopping cart gridlock at the "express" checkout	55
12	Being impatient with son	60
13	Asking parents for money	65
14	Being tired but still have to work	70
15	Not prepared for evening study group	75
16	Have to cancel outing with friends and they get mad	80
17	Car trouble on the interstate	85
18	Getting called in for work when I have other plans	90
19	Studying for statistics final exam	95
20	Son is sick and day care sends him home	100

Relaxation Procedure: Short Version with Five Muscle Groups

The relaxation exercise presented here is shorter than the exercise presented in Chapter 4. As you become proficient at the progressive muscle relaxation (PRT) exercise you can combine muscle groups and obtain the same level of relaxation as with the nine muscle group version (and, in fact, move to just 3 groups, and even down to the point where you can breathe and just tense your whole body and relax). The five muscle groups covered in this exercise are (1) hands and arms, (2) facial muscles forehead; eyes, nose, and cheeks; jaw, chin, front of neck, (3) back of the neck, (4) upper body, and (5) legs and feet. You may want to review the "before you begin" section from Chapter 4 for general tips on enhancing the effectiveness of the PRT exercise.

Progressive Muscle Relaxation: Short Version

(1) The first muscle group to work on is your hands and arms. With your thumbs on the outside, make a fist with your hand. At the same time, twist your arms around to create tension in your forearms **and** dig your elbows into the back of the chair to create tension in your upper arms. Notice the tension in your hands and arms. Focus in on this sensation of tension you are creating in your hands and arms. Now, all at once, relax your hands and forearms. Let the tension flow out. Notice the difference between the sensation of relaxation you feel in your arms right now and the sensation of tension that you created just moments ago. Focus on this difference. Take a deep slow breath ☺.

(2) Previously you learned to tense and relax the facial muscles in three separate groups. In this condensed version of the PRT exercise you will tense all the facial muscles at once (forehead; eyes, nose, and cheeks; jaw, chin, front of neck). If you think that it would be difficult to arch your eyebrows at the same time that you are shutting your eyes tightly, as would be required if we just combined the three facial muscle groups, you are right. To tense all the facial muscles at once you want to *furrow* your eyebrows by drawing them down towards your eye and in towards the middle of your forehead and tightly shut your eyes. At the same time crinkle up your nose by pulling up your nose toward your eyes. Finally, while biting down on the teeth in the back of your mouth, try to pull the corners of your mouth down into an exaggerated clown frown (looks like this ☹). Focus on the tension you are creating. Feel that band of tension across your forehead, the tension in your eyes, nose, and cheeks, and notice the tension through your jaw, chin and through the front of you neck. Now, all at once, relax your facial muscles. Let your eyebrows relax, let your jaw go slack, and let all the muscles in your face feel completely relaxed. Notice the difference between the sensation of relaxation you feel in your face now and the sensation of tension you had created just moments ago. Focus on that difference.

Progressive Muscle Relaxation: Short Version (Continued)

(3) The next area to work on is the shoulders and neck and you will tense and relax these muscles just as you did in the longer version of this exercise. Pull your chin down into your Adam's apple until it almost touches your chest. Feel the tension you are creating in your neck. Focus on this tension. Now, all at once, relax your neck, let it loose. Notice the difference between the sensation of relaxation you feel now and the sensation of tension you created just moments ago. Focus on this difference. Take in a deep slow breath ☺.

(4) The fourth muscle group is the mid-body area. Again, you will tense and relax these muscles just as you did in the longer version of this exercise. While taking in a slow breath, draw your shoulders back and try to make your shoulder blades touch. Now arch your back. Hold this position until you have to exhale and then exhale slowly, letting the tension flow out as you relax. Notice the difference between the sensation of relaxation you feel now and the sensation of tension you created in this area just moments ago. Focus on that difference and breathe deeply.

(5) The legs and feet are the final muscle group. You will be using one of the leg exercises from the full length exercise. Raise your legs up and hold them in front of you. You should feel tension through your thighs and hamstrings and buttocks. At the same time point your toes up towards the ceiling and back toward you so that you create tension all through your calves and shins. Feel the sensation of tension that you are creating. Now, relax your legs and let them fall to the floor. Notice the difference between the sensation of relaxation you feel in your legs now and the sensation of tension you had created in it just moments ago. Focus on this difference. Breathe very deeply and very slowly ☺.

Visualization

Once you are relaxed you can use the visualization exercises to deepen your level of relaxation and enhance your imagery of events from your stressful events hierarchy. The visualization exercise below follows the relaxation exercise and prepares you for the actual imagery rehearsal with your stressful events hierarchy.

After you have tensed and relaxed your legs and feet go back through your muscles in your imagination and allow each muscle to relax even more. Remember, as each part of you relaxes, all of you relaxes more deeply, and as you relax more deeply, each part can relax even more easily. Now imagine a triangle in your mind's eye...any type of triangle will do... you may imagine you see it on a screen, like a movie or television screen, or you may imagine it in your mind...just notice which is easier for you...notice what type of triangle you see...notice if the image is steady and vivid, or if it comes and goes, or changes as you watch it...remember, it doesn't really matter how you imagine it...just stay relaxed and observe what is happening....

If you'd like the image to be clearer or more vivid imagine you have a set of controls like a remote for your TV set, and experiment with them until the image is the way you want it...or just take a couple of deep breaths and relax more deeply as you let them go, letting the image become clearer as you do...notice how these techniques work for you....

Let that image fade and imagine a circle...notice how big or small it is, and how round...let the circle be yellow...a bright yellow circle...notice if it helps to think of the sun or a yellow lemon...let the yellow fade and imagine the circle is red...like an apple or red bouncing ball...now let that go and imagine that the circle is blue...like the sky or the ocean....

Let that image go...Take a moment and scan your body imagining it full of tiny blinking red lights...from your hands up your arms...to your shoulders...your face, eyes, nose, ears...to your jaw and neck...down your back...to your hips and thighs...down your calves to the tips of your toes...your body is filled with red Christmas lights...notice which parts of your body are very relaxed...and imagine those lights dimming and turning blue...notice where the red lights are still blinking...use your set of controls to dim those lights to blue...or take a few deep breaths...focusing on allowing those muscles to become even more relaxed...and notice how the lights turn blue...your body is completely relaxed and just watch the blue lights blinking on and off.

Now let that go...and recall some time you felt very much at peace with yourself...a time when you felt very peaceful, very centered and calm...imagine it as if it were happening right now...notice where you are...and who you're with...what you're doing...notice your posture...and your face...especially notice the feelings of peacefulness and centeredness in you...notice where you feel these qualities, and let them be there...let them begin to grow in you...let them expand and get bigger, filling your whole body with feelings of peacefulness and calm....

Imagery Rehearsal: Application

Now you are ready to vividly imagine yourself in the first situation (SUDs=5) on your stressful events hierarchy. Start with external imagery, imagining yourself in the situation as if you were a spectator (Chapter 7 discusses internal and external imagery in more detail). As you watch yourself in the situation take note of any signs of tension in your body and apply your relaxation skills and deep breathing to relax those areas. Now change your imagery of the situation to the internal perspective. Instead of watching yourself as a spectator would, imagine yourself in the situation so that you see the situation through your own eyes. Feel yourself move rather than watch yourself move. If you look down at your feet you should be able to see the front of your body but not your back. Vividly imagine yourself in the stressful situation, notice when you begin to feel to tense, and imagine coping with that situation using your positive coping statements. Breathe. If tension persists while imagining a scene from the hierarchy, clear your mind of the stressful scene and substitute a relaxing image. If needed, use the PRT exercise to relax your body. Move to the next hierarchy scene only after twice remaining totally relaxed for about 20 seconds while vividly imagining the previous scene. As you move up the hierarchy some scenes will require more repetitions than others. Go at your own pace. If you practice a scene more than six times and are not able to use your coping statements and deep breathing to stay relaxed, you may want to review your hierarchy and see if the troublesome scene might actually have a higher SUDS rating than you initially assigned it.

<u>How Does it Work?</u>   Imagery rehearsal helps you overcome anxiety in two ways. First, simply teaching yourself to be relaxed while imagining the stressful scene serves to counter the anxiety. You are using classical conditioning procedures when you pair relaxation with a particular situation. This aspect of imagery rehearsal is similar to systematic desensitization. While pairing relaxation with the stressful scenes helps diminish the physiological arousal elicited by the stressful situation, visualizing the use of positive coping statements alters the arousal eliciting thoughts that accompany the situation. Moreover, it is thought that this type of imaginal practice has the same performance enhancing effects as observed among athletes using visualization to learn and practice new skills and hence improve their performance (Chapter 7).

REVIEW OF STEPS IN IMAGINED REHEARSAL

1. Relax your body with a short version of PRT.

2. Do a few "warm-up" visualization exercises while relaxed.

3. Vividly imagine yourself in the first situation (SUDs of 5) on your hierarchy. Enhance your image of the scene by taking note of all of your sensory impressions (sights, sounds, smells, tastes, touch). As you are in the situation visualize yourself actually using the positive coping statements you developed for this particular situation. Hold onto this scene for 30 to 40 seconds. Take note of any tension in your body and apply PRT and deep breathing to relax those areas.

4. After you have twice been able to remain relaxed while vividly imagining the first scene for about 20 seconds, move on to the next scene in the hierarchy.

5. Continue this process with each scene in the hierarchy.

6. Success in this exercise requires attention and concentration, therefore it is a good idea to work through only 3 or 4 events at a time.

7. When you get to the top of the hierarchy in imagined rehearsal you are ready to **practice in real life**. Actively plan to use your new coping skills in situations low on your stressful event hierarchy and gradually move to more difficult situations.

Overcoming Roadblocks

After reading through the chapter for the first time you may think that the program seems too complicated, or you may feel like it would take you the rest of your life to complete all the steps. If you are apprehensive about the program for these reasons, here are few points that should help allay your concerns.

Overcoming Roadblocks and Getting the Most From SIT

<u>1</u>. SIT includes a whole array of techniques that *you choose* from in order to help with your particular problem. You do not have to use every technique reviewed in the beginning of this chapter. SIT offers you flexibility and encourages you to experiment and discover for yourself what works and doesn't work well for you.

<u>2</u>. The one aspect of SIT that has not already been covered in previous chapters involves Imagery Rehearsal. Although there are numerous steps involved in imagery rehearsal, the procedure actually proceeds fairly quickly. Generating your list of stressful events (including noting salient sensory cues), assigning SUDs scores, and arranging them in a hierarchy probably will not take more than 45 minutes. Its OK if you have less than 20 items and the increment between items does not have to be exactly five. Developing positive coping statements for each situation is also about a 45 minute task. Basically you can have your hierarchy and coping statements developed in an hour and a half or less. Becoming relaxed and beginning the imagery exercises is a 10-15 minute exercise and each session of actually visualizing yourself using the positive coping statements should last no longer than 15 minutes. You will probably need to have 5-7 sessions of these relaxation and visualization sessions to reach the top of the hierarchy and you may want to repeat the hierarchy once to reinforce your success. When you add up the total amount of time its a relatively small amount of time. If you practice twice a day you could be ready for "real life" practice in 1-2 weeks. Breaking tasks down into manageable units is always a useful technique to manage seemingly overwhelming tasks.

Chapter 11

Assertiveness Training

Background: What is Assertive Behavior?

Assertive behavior is interpersonal behavior which involves the honest, straightforward, direct and effective expression of feelings. Assertiveness training is a direct action stress management technique from which almost everyone can profit to some extent. Few of us meet our own expectations for effective assertive behavior in <u>all</u> of the different types of interpersonal situations we encounter. Most of us find certain people (e.g., mom or dad, your boss, your teachers) or certain situations (e.g., making requests, turning down requests, expressing opinions) inhibiting or intimidating. The following are examples of some specific situations that require assertive behavior and that result in increased stress levels if one is exposed to them repeatedly and is unable to deal with them assertively.

Typical Situations Associated with Unassertive Behavior and Negative Emotion

- Becoming embarrassed and flustered when someone gives you a compliment.

- Feeling angry when the food at a restaurant is poor but not saying anything to the waitperson because you do not want to "make a fuss"

- Wanting to be someone that friends and family "can count on" but feeling overwhelmed, and perhaps resentful, by all the demands being made on your time.

- Wanting to ask for a raise or promotion that you feel you deserve but not being able to find the words and feeling overwhelmed by anxiety.

- Going along with your friends' preferences when you would rather do something else.

The possibility of conflict arising from asserting oneself makes some people very anxious and they reduce their tension by remaining quiet or by "giving in." When people are repeatedly confronted with interpersonal situations that they find overwhelming and in which they are unable to assert themselves they find themselves under chronically high levels of stress.

Distinguishing Between Assertive, Aggressive and Passive Behavior

Many people who are passive are reluctant to be assertive because they fear their behavior will be perceived as aggressive. People who are aggressive often fear that a lack of aggression on their part will be perceived as passivity. Assertive behavior is the desired middle ground but how can you tell which is which?

Assertive Behavior. The goal of assertive behavior is to honestly, effectively, and directly express your thoughts, feelings, wants and beliefs. With assertive behavior you stand up for your rights while respecting the rights of others.

Aggressive Behavior. The goal of aggressive behavior is to dominate, hurt, humiliate, denigrate, and manipulate (although the person behaving aggressively may be unaware of this). With aggressive behavior a person stands up for their rights at the expense of other people. The end of this chapter presents conflict management techniques which are useful direct action techniques for transforming aggressive behavior into assertive behavior.

Passive Behavior. The goal of passive behavior is to please others, avoid conflict, be perceived by others as a nice person, and hide one's feelings. With passive behavior people do not express what is on their mind and they do not stand up for their legitimate rights. As a result, they often have their rights trampled on by others. This can lead to "bottled-up" anger and resentment (anger-in) that periodically manifests itself in an explosion of verbal and/or physical aggressive behavior.

Where Does Unassertive (Passive) Behavior Come From?

Unassertive behavior is a learned pattern of interacting with other people. Everyone has different experiences which account for how they learned to be unassertive in particular situations but there are some common themes that help explain a great deal of the unassertive behavior you may observe in yourself and others.

1. Punishment. Unassertive behavior sometimes develops because assertive behavior was punished in the past. For example, you may be afraid to express your opinion with your current friends, in part because your friends in grade school made fun of your opinions. Similarly, your parents may have given you the message that the appropriate way to behave was "don't rock the boat" or "don't speak until spoken to." Expressing opinions or show of initiative may have been punished with a frown, a verbal rebuke, or even a spanking to let you know it was inappropriate.

2. Positive Reinforcement. Unassertive behavior is often positively reinforced making it more likely that you will be unassertive in the future. For example, you may agree to do things you do not want to do, or do not have time for, because your friends shower you with compliments.

3. Negative Reinforcement. Negative reinforcement also helps to maintain unassertive behavior by allowing us to avoid unpleasant negative arousal. Specifically, unassertive (passive) behavior is a form of avoidance behavior. Avoiding potential conflict and disagreement eliminates negative arousal. The anxiety that you may feel when contemplating behaving assertively is triggered when what you want or need (e.g., a raise at work; help with the dishes at home) is in conflict with your irrational beliefs (e.g, I must never be rejected; I must be perfect).

4. Modeling. We learn a great deal of our behavior patterns by observing and imitating the behavior of others in our environment who control reinforcers, have prestige and are admired by others. For most of us our most important models are our parents. If one of your parents was/is unassertive in their interactional style, it is likely that you picked up some of those same patterns from them (e.g., perhaps your mom never voiced her opinions and tried to be the perfect mother/housewife).

Assertiveness Training Procedures

Clearly, thoughts, feelings and actions all interact and feed off of each other to produce unassertive behavior. Typically when a person is unassertive, anxiety (feelings) prevents them from behaving assertively (avoidant actions) because they have unrealistic beliefs (thoughts) about what will happen if they behave assertively. Passive behavior (avoidant actions) may result in reduced anxiety (feelings) but continual failure to have your rights respected and feelings expressed often leads to anger and resentment (feelings) which can "leak" out in aggressive behavior (actions) such as sarcastic or hurtful verbal behavior or explode in angry tirades or even physical aggression. The assertiveness training procedures which follow encourage you to use several of the building block chapters to increase your skills at regulating your emotions and changing your maladaptive beliefs before tackling the direct action portion of the intervention.

1. Emotion Focused Coping. Proficiency at deep breathing and relaxation from Chapters 2 and 4 are essential in order to effectively reduce tension and anxiety to manageable levels in situations where you plan to try your new assertive behavior. You may also find some of the techniques in Chapters 7- 9 useful for regulating the negative emotion associated with your particular assertiveness problem.

2. Changing Maladaptive Thoughts. Chapter 5 covers the fundamental skills pertaining to changing unrealistic thoughts and beliefs. It is important that you be able to identify those beliefs (e.g., everybody must like me) which contribute to your anxiety and avoidance of assertive behavior. You do not need to be an expert at refuting your maladaptive beliefs to proceed with the assertiveness exercises but you should have some experience practicing the refuting exercises.

3. Self Assessment. Use a structured diary from Chapter 3 to identify the situations in which you have problems being assertive. Examine the Assertiveness Self-Assessment Table on the following page to help clarify the types of situations you find most problematic. Review the information from both sources and look for common themes. As you can see from the accompanying table some typical problem areas include Expressing Positive Feelings (giving and receiving compliments, making requests, expressing liking and affection, making conversation), Self-Affirmation (standing up for your rights, refusing requests, expressing personal opinions), and Expressing Negative Feelings (annoyance, displeasure, anger).

Once you have identified common the general areas where you have difficulty being assertive select a specific area to target for change. Generally, it is better to start with easier areas first (areas that are less, rather than most anxiety provoking and difficult) and tackle more difficult areas as your confidence and skill level increase. Make sure your structured diary includes examples where you were appropriately assertive. You want to assess your strengths as well as weaknesses and build on your strengths in this exercise.

Excerpted and condensed from Galassi, M.D., & Galassi, J.P. (1977). <u>Assert Yourself! How to Be Your Own Person.</u> Plenum Publishing: New York.

ASSESSING YOUR BEHAVIOR

You learned that assertive behavior involves directly expressing your feelings, preferences, needs rights, and opinions without undue anxiety and in a manner that is neither threatening nor punishing to others. However, before learning more about behaving assertively, it would be helpful to determine how you presently express yourself. Self-assessment provides information that is helpful in tailoring the program to meet the your specific needs. An Assertion Self-Assessment Table is on the next page. Detach it from the manual and follow the simple step-by-step instructions listed below.

Frequency of Asserting Yourself

Step 1. In reading the table, use the following question with each row and column heading: Do I *(row heading)* to/from/of/with *(column heading)* when it is appropriate?

Example: Do I *give compliments* to *friends of the same sex* when it is appropriate?

Step 2. In answering the question for each cell, write in the word which best describes how often you engage in the behavior in that situation. Choose the most appropriate answer from the words *usually, sometimes,* or *seldom.*

Step 3. Now complete each cell in the table as described in Steps 1 and 2.

Step 4. Notice wherever you answered with the words *seldom* and *sometimes.* We suggest that you devote special attention to these behaviors when you design your assertion training program.

Step 5. Again, notice wherever you answered with the words *seldom* or *sometimes.* Are there one or more persons for whom you have given a number of *seldom* and *sometimes* answers. We suggest that you devote special attention to these persons when you design your assertion training program.

Step 6. For some people, *seldom* and *sometimes* answers do not group into any particular behaviors or persons. This is not uncommon. If you are one of those people, you will have to select the most relevant discussion and exercise modules from the manual when you design your assertion training program.

Step 7. Assess whether you experience any discomfort or undue anxiety when you express yourself. Use the following question with each row and column heading: When I *(row heading)* to/from/of/with *(column heading)*, do I become very nervous of unduly anxious?

Example.: When I *give compliments* to *friends of the same sex,* do I become very nervous or unduly anxious?

Step 8. For each cell, answer the question with either a *yes* or *no*. If you answer *yes*, write *yes* in the cell. However, if you answer *no*, do not write it in the cell.

Step 9. Now complete each cell in the table as described in Steps 7 and 8.

Step 10. Look at the table and note where you entered the word *yes*. Include those behaviors in your assertion training program, you may want to incorporate relaxation training.

Step 11. Again, look at the table and note where you entered the word *yes*. Include those persons in your assertion training program, you may want to incorporate relaxation training.

Step 12. For some people, *yes* answers do not group into any particular behaviors or persons. This is not uncommon, since people often experience anxiety only when expressing certain feelings to certain people.

Step 13. If you are considering assertion training because you feel that your behavior is aggressive at times, continue with Steps 14-19. If this is not a concern of yours, skip over these steps.

Step 14. Assess whether you experience any aggression when you express yourself. Use the following question with each row and column heading: Am I aggressive when I *(row heading)* to/from/of/with *(column heading)*?

Example: Am I aggressive when I *express justified anger* to *co-workers*?

Step 15. In answering the question for each cell, *shade* in those cells for which you report behaving aggressively in that situation.

Step 16. Complete each cell as described in Steps 14 and 15.

Step 17. Look at the table and note the cells you shaded. Are there particular behaviors for which you have shaded a number of cells? Include those behaviors in your assertion training program.

Step 18. Again, look at the table and note the cells you shaded. Are there particular persons for whom you have shaded a number of cells? Include those persons in your assertion training program.

Step 19. For some people, shaded cells do not group under any particular behaviors or persons. This is not uncommon, since people often are aggressive only when expressing certain feelings to certain people.

TABLE 1
Assertion of Self-Assessment Table

Persons

Behaviors	Friends of the same sex	Friends of the opposite sex	Intimate relations, e.g., spouse, boyfriend, girlfriend	Parents, in-laws, and other family members	Children	Authority figures, e.g., bosses, professors, doctors	Business contacts, e.g., sales-persons, waiters	Co-workers, colleagues, and sub-ordinates
Expressing Positive Feelings Give compliments								
Receive Compliments								
Make requests, e.g., ask for favors, help, etc.								
Express liking, love, and affection								
Initiate and maintain conversations								
Self-Affirmation Stand up for your legitimate rights								
Refuse requests								
Express personal opinions including disagreement								
Expressing Negative Feelings Express justified annoyance and displeasure								
Express justified anger								

4.   Define the Problem. Use W questions as you review your structured diary to define the problem in concrete, specific terms focusing on what is factual, not opinion or emotion.

Who is involved?

Where does it happen?

When does it happen?

Why, as you understand it, does it happen?

What are your thoughts, actions, and feelings?

What happens that is bothersome?

What needs and wants are being thwarted?

What goals are in conflict?

5.   Plan Direct Action. Use the D_E_S_C system to plan your assertive encounter.

D-Describe the other person's behavior that is a concern for you

E-Express what you feel and think about this behavior

S-Specify explicitly what changes you would like in this behavior

C-Consequences-Spell out the consequences to both of you if your concern is or is not resolved.

In the initial stages of this exercise it is important to actually plan and write out how you would like to express yourself assertively in your selected situation. As you become more proficient at assertiveness you will be able to go through these steps automatically in spontaneous interpersonal situations that arise throughout the day.

6.   An Example of the DESC Script

John has recurring unpleasant encounters with his parents who he describes as loving and caring but also nosy and pushy. His parents frequently ask him about his "love life" and question whether his decision to major in psychology is very smart when he would have a more secure career path majoring in finance and joining the family business upon graduation like his brother did. John loves his parents but he dreads their phone calls. Last time they called his mom got on the phone first and asked him if he was "seeing anyone special." John would usually reply to this question with something innocuous like "no one as special as you mom" and then clam up and end the conversation. But that night he had enough and snapped back in anger "Mom you are always being a busy body nosing into my personal affairs. Why don't you mind your own business for a change and leave me alone. Believe me, you will be the last person to know when I start seeing someone special." This emotional and personal attack on his mother was completely out of character for John. Unfortunately, this type of building resentment and eventual aggressive outburst is not uncommon for people who are unassertive. Below is an example of how John might have used the DESC script to develop an assertive response to his mother's inquiries that would have achieved his goals and would also have respected the rights and feelings of his mother.

DESC Example

DESCRIBE	Mom, the last three times you called you asked me if I was seeing someone special.
EXPRESS	I think you are just concerned about my happiness and well being but it makes me feel uncomfortable when you ask me these types of personal questions.
SPECIFY	Please don't ask me about my love life anymore.
CONSEQUENCES	I think we will both enjoy our conversations more if the conversation did not focus on this part of my life.

In this DESC script John described the problem in the here and now. He does not go back twenty years and recite a whole litany of examples of his mother's "nosy" behavior. He is not trying to get his mother to correct all of her past sins in one assertive encounter, rather he is just trying to change one current behavior pattern that he finds problematic. He expressed himself with "I" statements that reflected how he feels and thinks and avoids accusations and personal attacks. He specified clearly and politely exactly what he wanted and he described the pleasant consequences that they would both enjoy if she would comply with his request.

Fill in the table below to describe an assertive response John might make towards his father when dad calls and starts pressuring John to change his major.

DESCRIBE	
EXPRESS	
SPECIFY	
CONSEQUENCES	

7.   Assertiveness in Real Life. Use the DESC script to prepare for an assertive encounter that is personally relevant to you. After you have prepared your DESC script rehearse the assertive encounter in your own mind. Make sure to use the deep breathing exercise both in your rehearsal and in your real life assertive encounter. There are several other techniques covered in this book that you may find helpful in preparing for an assertive encounter (Visualization, Controlling Anticipatory Anxiety, Stress Inoculation Training), however, do not use review of these materials as an excuse to avoid the encounter. If you have progressed through steps 1-7 above you are ready to practice in real life. **Go and do it.** Note in your structured diary how the encounter went, how you felt, what were the outcomes. As you increase your confidence begin to implement these same procedures in different types of situations.

To Be or Not to Be Assertive

To be or not to be; to act or not to act; these are the critical questions to be asked before implementing any of the direct action stress management techniques. With regard to assertive behavior some people believe that it is less stressful to just "go with the flow," or to just "grin and bear it." Some people reject the idea of being assertive because they believe that being assertive is "just not worth the trouble" it causes. In some situations the decision to not be assertive may well be the most adaptive response. However, most people who have these beliefs grossly underestimate their ability to change a situation in a positive direction by being more assertive. As we noted in Chapter 1, if it is true that your actions in fact are very unlikely to have an impact on the situation, if you in fact have no control, then it is probably better to use an emotion focused technique and/or take a different type of direct action (such as removing yourself from the situation) to reduce the stress you experience in an unpleasant but unchangeable situation. Some of the things the first author's clients have said in this regard exemplify the reasoning that people give for "deciding" not to be assertive.

Client 1
"I can't stand the way my boss treats me but I'm only going to be in the job another 6 months, why rock the boat now?" "He will just get mad if I say something and make my life even more miserable."

Client 2
"The S.O.Bs. cheated me out of my last pay check but I am making good money now, why bother to pursue it?"

Client 3
"All I want the man to do is help watch the kids so I can cook dinner. I don't say anything to him but he should know that I need help. But does he offer to help when he gets home. **NOOooo**. He just comes home from work and plops himself down and acts like I am the maid around this joint or something."

Are these clients being realistic or are they rationalizing away their difficulties with being assertive? How can you tell if you are in a situation where you would be better off if you were assertive, rather than unassertive like these three clients above? You must weigh the pros and cons for yourself and decide whether to take direct action or not, but we have a few points for you to consider to guide your decision-making process. Remember, to do nothing is to decide to be passive. If you are going to be unassertive in a situation you will probably feel better and more in control if you actively weigh the pros and cons and make a concrete decision, and a plan of action, to cope with the stress of the situation in another manner.

Guidelines for Deciding Whether or Not to be Assertive

1. Realize that most people grossly exaggerate the potential for negative outcomes in situations where they contemplate assertive action. A common belief is that others will not like you if you behave assertively. Research has disproved this belief and has actually provided data to suggest just the opposite. Most people would rather be with an assertive person than an unassertive person. It is very frustrating to be with someone who will not express their preferences. For example, consider the sometimes endless round robin of trying to figure out where to go out to eat or what movie to see when one or more people in a group will only say "whatever you want" when asked their preference. Most people would rather not have to be a mind reader to find out what you want, like, and need.

2. It is important to track your level of negative arousal (e.g., anxiety, resentment, anger, frustration) not only in the situation but after the situation as well. You may feel better initially if you avoid an assertive encounter because avoidance behavior removes you from the anxiety/stressful situation. However, if in the long term your level of anger and resentment builds you probably want to reconsider an assertive response to the situation.

3. If you are unassertive because you are in a physically abusive relationship and a change in your behavior will clearly have negative consequences then use a different direct action strategy. Namely leave the situation, rather than try assertiveness.

Chapter 12

Social Skills Training

Background: What are Social Skills?

Social skills can be defined as specific learned behaviors that an individual uses during social interactions to solicit reinforcing responses from others. These behaviors can be verbal or non verbal. Reinforcement for the particular behavior can be a good conversation, a job interview resulting in employment, and even landing a hot date for Saturday night. How do social skills differ form assertiveness skills?

Chapter 11 discussed in detail assertiveness skills, which are a specific category of social skills. This chapter will present a variety of practice exercises to enhance your repertoire of more general social skills. For example understanding the importance of non verba behavior, conversational skills, date initiation skills all fall under the rubric of social skills. As you learned in the assertiveness chapter, often times people have the requisite skills (assertiveness or social skills) but do not use them in a particular situation because of their maladaptive beliefs and anxiety in the situation. Often people have the skills but are afraid to use them because they fear rejection, humiliation, etc. Chapter 11 on assertiveness is full of such examples and discusses how to use the chapters presented earlier in the book to help lower emotional arousal in the situation and change maladaptive beliefs before actually using the assertiveness skills per se. This chapter takes a somewhat different approach. We assume that you already able to apply the emotional regulation techniques you have learned as well the techniques for identifying and changing maladaptive beliefs that inhibit your use of social skills (e.g., date initiation skills). Therefore, this chapter focuses on developing actual behaviors through observation, rehearsal and actual practice.

Completing the Social Avoidance Stress Scale in the box below will give you some information regarding how strong your anxiety is in social situations. If you score moderately or very high on this scale you probably want to include an emotional regulation and cognitive intervention to the ones presented here in this chapter.

Social Avoidance Distress Scale

Answer TRUE or FALSE after each statement as it applies to **you**

1. I feel relaxed even in unfamiliar social situations.
2. I try to avoid situations which force me to be very sociable.
3. It's easy for me to relax when I am with strangers.
4. I have no particular desire to avoid people.
5. I often find social occasions upsetting.
6. I usually feel calm and comfortable at social occasions.
7. I am usually at ease when talking to someone of the opposite sex.
8. I try to avoid talking to people unless I know them well.
9. If the chance comes to meet new people, I often take it.
10. I often feel nervous and tense in casual get-togethers in which both sexes are present.
11. I am usually nervous with people unless I know them well.
12. I usually feel relaxed when I am with a group of people.
13. I often want to get away from people.
14. I usually feel uncomfortable when I am in a group of people I don't know.
15. I usually feel relaxed when I meet someone for the first time.
16. Being introduced to people makes me tense and nervous.
17. Even though a room is full of strangers, I may enter it any way.
18. I would avoid walking up and joining a large group of people.
19. When my superiors want to talk with me, I talk willingly.
20. I often feel on edge when I am with a group of people.
21. I tend to withdraw from people.
22. I don't mind talking to people at parties or social gatherings.
23. I am seldom at ease in a large group of people.
24. I often think up excuses in order to avoid social engagements.
25. I sometimes take the responsibility for introducing people to each other.
26. I try to avoid formal social occasions.
27. I usually go to whatever social engagements I have.
28. I find it easy to relax with other people.

Answers 1)f 2)t 3)f 4)f 5)t 6)f 7)f 8)t 9)f 10)t 11)t 12)f 13)t 14)t 15)f 16)t 17)f 18) t 19)f 20)t 21)t 22)f 23)t 24)t 25)f 26)t 27)f 28)f. Add the number of items that you answered in the direction indicated. Scores above 14 suggest moderately high levels of social anxiety.

How do we acquire social skills?

Observing the behavior of others is one of the most important ways in which we acquire social skills. Whether or not we choose to emulate the behavior of others depends on several factors. As noted by Jeffery A. Kelley, Ph.D., an expert in the area of social skills, these factors include; the age of the observed person (model), sex of the model, whether or not the model is amiable, whether or not there are any perceived similarities between the observer and the model, whether or not the model is rewarded or punished for the behavior, and whether the exhibited behavior is similar to any of the observer's prior behaviors. The models for social behavior are not limited to those persons close in proximity. Television personalities as well as other fictional characters have an influence on social behavior. It will be important for you to identify people in your environment who vary in their level of social skills. You will be observing these people in order to improve your ability to identify (and emulate) behavior (both verbal and nonverbal) that is socially skilled. That is, the behaviors of others that seem to lead to the types of reinforcements you want (more friends, a date, a job, etc).

Feedback is another aspect in the development of social skills. Feedback is the positive or negative information one receives in response to his or her behavior that can be used as an evaluative tool to adjust one's own behavior. Feedback can be a direct statement, "I didn't think you were listening because you would not look at me" or nonverbal cues such as increased or decreased eye contact. The feedback needs to be detectable in order to be of use. Learning to pick up on some of the more subtle cues can be extremely helpful in social situations. In the next section of this chapter you will practice identifying the meaning of nonverbal cues, observe these cues in others, and practice deliberately using non-verbals in your daily social interactions.

Nonverbal Behaviors

We use nonverbal behaviors every day without really giving it much thought. How many of us "speak with our hands" or have heard someone say, "it was written all over your face"? These are examples of nonverbals. The following is a list of nonverbal behaviors that we use and see everyday.

Match the Term on the Left with its Example on the Right

1. <u>Gaze</u>-   a. staring, looking past someone, looking up, etc.

2. <u>Gestures</u>-   b. whisper, raspy, loud, mellow, soft

3. <u>Head Movements</u>-   c. toward or away from you

4. <u>Facial Expressions</u>-   d. waving hands, making fist, flipping the bird

5. <u>Voice Tone & Volume</u>-   e. how near or far another person is from you

6. <u>Interpersonal Distance</u>-   f. nods, shaking head

7. <u>Body Orientation</u>-   g. smile, frown, raised eyebrows

answers)a 2)d 3)f 4)g 5)b 6)e 7)c

That was easy. Now, to increase your awareness of the nonverbal behavior further, complete the listing exercise below.

List the Nonverbals Associated with Each of the Items Below			
Happy		Asking a Question	
Angry		Scolding Someone	
Sick		Praising Someone	
Surprised		Scared	
Relaxed		Lost	

Being aware of the interplay between nonverbal and verbal behavior in daily conversation is a key social skill. We send messages and have the opportunity to pick up more information when we are sensitive to both channels of communication. Read over the table below of common nonverbal behaviors and how they can be used to enhance (or detract from) a conversation. When we are aware of another persons non verbal behavior our opportunity to respond and interact with the person is greatly expanded. For example, if you initiate a conversation with "high how are you" and the other person says "fine" the conversation can easily dry up with just those two sentences. However, if you have become astute at reading nonverbal cues you might keep the conversation going with something like "gee you seem anxious" or tired, or angry, etc., whatever the emotional undertone conveyed by the "fine" response. When we are empathic with people in this way, others usually respond to us in a more positive manner. The key though is to be able to accurately identify the meanings of the non-verbals and respond in a sincere and honest manner.

Common Nonverbal Behaviors	
GAZE	Used to Show Interest or Disinterest
GESTURES	Clarifies or Emphasizes a Statement; Asks a Question; Gives Direction
Head Movements	Can Indicate Agreement, Disagreement, Attention
Facial Expression	Express Emotion; Asks a Question; Emphasize a Point
Voice Tone & Volume	Used to Indicate a Question; Clarify or Emphasize a Point
Posture	Sign of Comfort Level and Level of Interest

Homework Exercise: Observe (without staring) at two separate conversations among individuals. Notice and record their nonverbal behaviors and what you think might be going on in the conversations. Allow at least five minutes for each exercise.

CONVERSATION #1

NONVERBALS OBSERVED	MESSAGE BEING CONVEYED
1.	1.
2.	2.
3.	3.
4.	4.
5.	5.
6.	6.
7.	7.
8.	8.
9.	9.

CONVERSATION # 2

NONVERBALS OBSERVED	MESSAGE BEING CONVEYED
1.	1.
2.	2.
3.	3.
4.	4.
5.	5.
6.	6.
7.	7.
8.	8.
9.	9.

Initiating Conversation

There are as many ways to start a conversation as there are people in the world. We all however, need one thing in order to start a conversation, and that is the other person's attention. We use verbals ("Where did you find cool that shirt?") and non-verbals (a tap on the shoulder) to grab the attention of another individual. What are some of the ways you could nonverbally initiate conversation?

Nonverbals?_____

_____

_____

And verbally?_____

_____

_____

Often times we use a combination of both verbal and nonverbal behaviors. For instance, a woman points to another woman's purse and says, "Where did you find such a beautiful purse?"

How would you start an interaction?
(use both verbals and nonverbals)

1. You notice a person who reading a book by your favorite author. _____

_____

_____

2. You have been standing in line alone to ride a roller coaster for 45 minutes, you are bored and would love to talk to the person in front of you. _____

_____

_____

This sounds like a very simple task, but as mentioned earlier some people become anxious at the thought of speaking to other people. It may be helpful for you to refer back to Chapters 2, 4, 5, 7, 10, and 12. Chapter 10 on Stress Inoculation Training combines many of the techniques covered in the other chapters mentioned and may well be worth reviewing now. Most people can proceed with this chapter and be successful as long when you practice the exercises in "real life" you start with very easy situations first. You want to build you confidence and gradually allow your anxiety about social situations to dissipate as you meet and cope with increasingly difficult challenges.

What are some of the things about the situation, other person, or your own feelings that get in the way of initiating a conversation?

_____

_____

_____

_____

_____

Drawing from all of the techniques you have learned in this book, how could you overcome these roadblocks?_____

_____

_____

_____

Practice starting conversations in the mirror. Find the ways in which you are most comfortable approaching others. Notice your posture, tone of voice, facial expressions, and other nonverbals. Are there things you would change? Are there things you would do the same way you always have? Would you want to talk to you? When you can answer "yes" to that question go out and practice on other people.

Keeping a Conversation Going

Now that you know how to get someone's attention the new goal is to keep it. You can judge whether or not someone is listening to you through their "listening behavior." Listening behaviors are also called "minimal encouragements". We use these behaviors to encourage other people to continue talking to us. These too can be verbal or nonverbal in nature.

EXAMPLES:

Verbal: "That's great," "Go on," "un-huh," "Really?," etc.

Non-verbal: nodding your head, smiling, eye contact, body orientation

What clues would let you know the person you are talking to is listening to you?

_____

_____

_____

Which minimal encouragements do use most often in conversation?

_____

_____

_____

Notice which minimal encouragements people use when speaking to you. Do they change the subject? This is not necessarily something to get discouraged over. The person might not be comfortable with the *subject* matter at hand and wish to talk to *you* about something else.

Other Tools for Your Conversational "Bag of Tricks"

There are more techniques available to help you maintain a conversation. These include open-ended questions, reflective statements, parallel experiences, and changing the subject.

Open-Ended Questions

Open-ended questions are the opposite of closed-ended questions. Closed-ended questions elicit very short, to the point answers ("yes", "no", "maybe", "I don't know"). Open-ended questions allow the respondent to answer in an unstructured manner ("What do you think about the new dress code?") Because the responses are not necessarily short, this is a good way to maintain a conversation and transition effectively into other topics to discuss.

Turn the following closed-ended questions into open-ended questions.

Example:
"Are you hungry?" = "What kinds of foods do you enjoy eating?"

1. Do you shop at Wal-Mart? = _____

2. Is it raining? = _____

3. Are you going on vacation this summer? = _____

_____

4. Did you get a new car? = _____

Reflective Statements

Reflective statements acknowledge that you understand what the speaker is saying. They can reflect or "mirror" the speakers' statements or they can translate what the speaker has just said.

Examples:

        Speaker: "I rushed my dog to the vet thinking she had an injury only to find out she was in labor!"

        Listener (interpret/translate):   "I bet you were shocked to find out your dog was having puppies!"

        or (mirror):   "You went all the way to the vet and had no idea she was in labor?"

Write a reflective statement for each of the following remarks:

1. I fell off the horse and broke my leg.

_____

_____

2. I have worked in the same department for three years without a raise.

_____

_____

3. I loved the movie we saw last night. _____

_____

Reflective statements put the speaker in a position to carry the conversation further.

Parallel experiences

Parallel experiences point out similarities and differences between the listener and the speaker while still remaining within the general topic area.

Example:

        Speaker: I couldn't go to the movie because I had to study for a final.
        Listener: I couldn't go because my mother was sick.
        Listener: Sally and I got our studying done went to see the play at the commons. It was great. You will really enjoy it if you get a chance to see it.

Write a Parallel Experience for Each Situation.

1. I love the music at this party!_____

_____

2. I won a pair of shoes in the drawing._____

_____

3. My team won the tournament last year._____

_____

Changing the Topic

Someone you think might be interesting starts to talking to you about the mating habits of the wallaby. You know nothing about this and do not care to know anything about the subject. How can you gracefully change the subject without stepping on the other person's toes?

One way to change the subject would be to wait for a familiar phrase or word out of which you could formulate a question. Say for instance the person talking about the wallaby mentions Australia. Now you have an opportunity to ask a question about Australia that has nothing to do with wallabies ("I would love to go to Australia, is it as beautiful as people say?")

Another strategy for changing the subject is to simply tell the person that you are uncomfortable with the subject or you know nothing about the subject but would love to talk about something else.

Depending on your environment you could also use an incident outside of the conversation to change the topic. If you are at a party and someone falls in the pool you might say, "Did you see that guy fall in the pool? Do you think that hurt?"

Describe how you could change the topic in each of the situations below.

1. One of your friends has just finished a book in a subject you find extremely dull and wants to tell you all about it.

_____

_____

_____

2. The lady next door just got out of the hospital and wants to tell you all about how large her bill is, right down to the aspirin she took.

_____

_____

3. Your cousin feels she is the best singer in the family and is rambling on about singing in the family talent show next summer.

_____

_____

_____

These tools are valuable skills that can enhance your interactions with other people. The conversational skills we have covered can be used in a group setting as well as in one on one situation. In time, as you have used and practiced these skills, they will become second nature.

Conversational Skills to Help You Get a Date

Date-initiation skills are very similar to other conversational skills. The main difference between date-initiation skills and conversational skills is the intention of obtaining a future interaction. The conversation itself would be more affectionate verbally (personal compliments) as well as physically (touching the other person during conversation) and would not be suitable for use in everyday situations.

Making Requests. We have covered the basic conversational skills. One thing we will add to them in this section is making requests. Requesting a date can be an anxiety producing proposition. For example, asking your grocer for a pound of fish and asking a good-looking person out for a seafood dinner are two very different things. When the grocer is out of fish you just pick something else, but when you are turned down for a date you have to deal with rejection.

What kinds of behaviors are appropriate for making a request?
More than likely you will have been conversing with the intended "date" for a period of time before you decide to ask them out. Not very many people would accept an offer from a stranger that walked up to them in the library and said, "Would you like to get a pizza?" Keeping this in mind you need to initiate a conversation and use your conversational skills to maintain the interaction. Refer back to previous parts of this chapter if you need more practice with the skills. Remember to use nonverbal skills along with verbal skills. You may also want to use your breathing exercises to relax yourself prior to making the request.

When you make the request be specific about the place you wish to go and time you want to meet or pick up the other person.

Example:
You work at a restaurant every weekend with a waiter/waitress you would like to go out with. You are both closing this evening so you decide to ask him/her out for a cup of coffee.

The other person says: I am ready to relax and put my feet up.
You say: I am getting off work the same time you are and would like to relax

	too. How about going to the cafe around the corner for coffee?
Other person:	Either says "okay" or turns you down- "I am really tired tonight and need to go home and get some sleep, but thanks anyway."
You could:	Let it go at that. Decide to modify your request- "I am pretty tired too and probably shouldn't have coffee before I go to sleep. Would you like to meet me for coffee tomorrow before we go to work."
Other person:	Either agrees and you set up time and place or says no
You could:	Let it go at that or say- "Maybe some other time, goodnight."

You can always try again another time or find someone else to ask out.

How would you ask someone out in each of the following situations?

1. You see a guy/girl you would like to go out with in one of your classes. He/she is picking up his/her books that have just fallen all over the floor.

What nonverbals can you use?_____

_____

Verbals?_____

_____

_____

If you were turned down?

_____

_____

_____

2. There is person that you see every time you go to the gym that you want to ask out. You have an opportunity to ask him/her out when you are both riding an exercise bike. Think of the kinds of skills you can use in this situation. (e.g., Parallel Experiences)

_____

_____

_____

_____

If you were turned down?

_____

_____

How do you feel when you are turned down? Rejection may dredge up negative self statements. Chapters 5 and 8 of the workbook may help you deal with your feelings. While it may be no consolation at the time of rejection, there are very few if any people who have *never* been turned down. Behavioral persistence is probably the most important key to success. If you find yourself discouraged return to some of the easier exercises in this chapter (e.g., initiating a conversation) and review in earnest Chapter 5 on changing unrealistic thoughts and beliefs("I must be perfect," "Everybody must like me") and Chapter 10 on stress inoculation.

Chapter 13

Time Management

Background

You have probably heard someone say "Time flies" or "I wish I had more time." Do we actually have any way of controlling time? If we consider time to be the numbers we see on our watches or on our desks, then the answer is no. In fact, there are situations where time seems to speed up or slow down, often in the opposite direction we would like. For example, think about how short an hour seems when you are taking a statistics test as opposed to how long the hour seemed just the week before when the professor was lecturing. Why does the passage of time seem to vary depending on the situation? According to Einstein, time is nothing more than the sum of the events of our lives. How we experience time is a function of the meaning we ascribe to events in our lives. Therefore, if we approach time in terms of events and our subjective experiences of them, as opposed to numbers on a watch or a wall clock, then we realize that time management is in fact nothing more than managing and organizing these events.

A key principle often considered in time management is the Pareto Principle. This is the idea that 20 percent of the events in our lives make up 80 percent of what we set out to accomplish. The other 80 percent of the events we experience are directed at accomplishing the other 20 percent of our objectives. The inefficiency that characterizes this "other" 80 percent of our life events reflects a failure to prioritize. Therefore our "free" time often passes by out of our of control and frequently filled with the daily hassles that serve as the chronic background stressors in our lives.

Many books and chapters have been written to help people better manage their life events. The advice that can be found in these books reflects the diversity of opinion on what is optimal time-management. Some books provide advice on how to have a 48 hour day and emphasize cutting out all wasted time and motion. These books come across as advocating an exceptionally rigid prescription to time management where all time, work and leisure must be goal directed (e.g, eliminate time wasted in preparing and consuming beverages, eliminate reading that is unproductive such as the comics and most fiction, never be late, etc). Other writers take the opposite extreme. Time is not to managed but simply experienced. This is the go with the flow, enjoy the moment, stop and smell the roses perspective. In its extreme form this view suggests that using time to be goal oriented is really stress-inducing. Most of us would profit from time-management practices that fall between these two extremes. We want to accomplish short and long term goals and be able to enjoyable pleasurable (though not necessarily "productive") activities guilt free. We suggest that many people would profit by establishing what their current priorities are in life and assessing the extent to which their daily activities bring them closer to their goals. Certain events will clearly be of more value than others and these should take precedence in our everyday planning to have effective time management. The activities that follow are written with this type of person in mind.

Start by completing the time management scale below to learn how stressed out you are with time-management problems. Whether your score is high or low, everyone can profit from examining their life goals and assessing how their daily decisions about how to spend their time helps (prevents) them from reaching their goals.

Time Management Scale

For each of the items below indicate the extent to which the item applies to you.

0	1,2,3	4,5,6	7,8,9	10
Never	**Sometimes**	**Frequently**	**Most of the Time**	**Always**

_____1. I am indispensable. I find myself taking on various tasks because I am The only one that can do them.

_____2. Daily crisis take up all of my time. I have no time to do important things because I am too busy putting out fires.

_____3. I attempt to do too much at one time. I feel I can do it all, and I rarely say "no."

_____4. I feel unrelenting pressure, as if I am always behind and have no way to catch up. I am always rushing.

_____5. I am working habitually long hours, 10, 12, 14, even 18 hours a day; 5, 6, 7 days a week.

_____6. I constantly feel overwhelmed by demands and details, and feel as if I am having to do what I do not want to do most of the time.

_____7. I feel guilty about leaving work on time. I do not have sufficient time for rest or personal relationships. I take worries and problems home.

_____8. I constantly miss deadlines.

_____9. I am plagued by fatigue and listlessness with many slack hours of unproductive   activity.

_____10. I chronically vacillate between unpleasant alternatives.

Sum your score for the 10 items. Scores below 35 indicate that your stress level is probably not significantly affected by time pressure. Scores between 35 and 60 indicate that you would profit from time management techniques. Scores above 60 suggest that your life may feel dangerously out of control. Now is the time to take the time to reassess your life goals and prioritize your life tasks.

Reasons for Poor Time Management

If time management is so important to successful living, then why do so many people have difficulties with implementing the concept in their daily lives? The Table below list four of the primary reasons for time management problems. These are only some of the most common reasons people fail to manage their time well, and of course for some people several of these reasons occur at the same time and are interrelated.

```
Common Reasons for Poor Time
        Management

1. Maladaptive Beliefs
2. Difficulties with Assertiveness
3. Imbalance of Priorities
4. Anxiety/Procrastination
```

1. Maladaptive Beliefs. One reason people manage time poorly is that they have maladaptive beliefs about their time and the way in which they spend it. Many people believe that they "must" or "should" get the maximum number of events accomplished in a day, each and every day. These beliefs can lead to over commitment and feeling constantly frazzled. These beliefs also often lead to feelings of guilt when there is free time. The idea of "free" time is anathema to some people who cannot relax and enjoy the moment when its available because they feel like they "should" be doing something productive. The idea of getting the most out of life is adaptive, but becomes maladaptive when the person begins to plan so many events in a day that he or she begins to feel overwhelmed. A person may look at how much has been committed to for that day and recognize that there is no way to accomplish it all. Then, because events have not been prioritized, the person "freezes up" and is unable to get anything of importance accomplished.

2. Difficulties with Assertiveness. Another reason why many people have problems in the area of time management is their inability to say "No." As you learned in the chapter on assertiveness, maladaptive beliefs often play a role in passive unassertive behavior. People often have the maladaptive belief that if they say "No" to someone or something then they will be thought of as a selfish, careless person. As was discussed in the assertiveness chapter, learning to say "No" can be one of your greatest assets. As you are developing effective time management skills, you will see that one key is to be able to prioritize the various things you could do in a day. Doing things you do not really want to do because of your concerns about other people not liking you or thinking that you are selfish is often maladaptive. Learning to prioritize and say "No" to low priority demands on your time will be essential for successful time management.

3. Lack of Balance in Daily Living. Imbalance in our lives is another reason why persons fail to manage their time effectively. Quite often people develop problems with time management because they are neglecting or overemphasizing some area of their lives. Some people for instance, are involved in numerous athletic activities, often to the point that they neglect other aspects of their life such as work, school, and other relationships. Others are so wrapped up in meeting their social demands that they fail to remain in good physical condition or to take time for themselves. Still others indulge excessively in activities such as sleep, TV, talking on the phone, drinking with friends, so that they are unable to accomplish those things that would lead them to the goals to which they aspire but never seem to do much to reach. Often this comes from not having clearly delineated short and long term goals. This leads to spending inappropriate amounts of time in activities that are not of top priority. For instance, going to a movie with some friends is a fine thing to do, but it is poor time management when one decides to do this the night before a major exam.

4. Anxiety/Procrastination. A final reason for poor time management is procrastination. Procrastination, more than anything else, is one of the main problems that affects people with time management problems. Both the person who lives by the motto "Never do today what you can put off until tomorrow" to the person who indicated that most of the time "I am working habitually long hours, 10, 12, 14, even 18 hours a day; 5, 6, 7 days a week" (item 5 of the Time Management Scale) are likely procrastinating a great deal. Procrastination is a form of overt behavior, specifically overt behaviors that are low priority tasks that we engage in when we have high priority items to attend to. High priority items are often associated with anxiety and procrastination allows us to avoid the anxiety. The anxiety is typically a by product of maladaptive thoughts such as, "I shouldn't try because I might not fully succeed," "I am afraid to try, because I might make a mistake," "I can't start working on the paper until I am in the zone," and "I won't attempt anything unless I am perfect at it." Often times these thoughts, and the tension that is created by postponing working on high priority tasks, is so ingrained and habitual that we are scarcely aware of them. These maladaptive thoughts are counterproductive and lead to further procrastination. One way of combating these thoughts is to say to yourself, "Is it better to have nothing done on this paper or to have some of it done?" Obviously, if you have some of it done then you are in a better position to complete the paper at a later date.

What about those people who say (and many of these people are our students), "I do my best work under pressure, I like it that way, I do not need time management." Are these people self-deluded or are they handling their time efficiently by waiting to the last minute? As usual in psychology, whether this style is adaptive or maladaptive depends on the individual. Waiting to the last minute to meet a deadline usually raises the intensity of effort on a single high priority activity. When time is compressed we tend to eliminate the activities that are low priority. In this sense people often do work best under pressure as long as the pressure is of moderate intensity. But do not confuse this with "your best work." What many people report when they complete a task to meet a deadline at the last minute is something along the lines of "this would have been really good if I just had a few more days." So, adaptive or maladaptive? How can you tell. If *you choose* to wait to the last minute to work on a task that is middle to low priority <u>and</u> can do so without excessive anxiety or guilt and this behavioral style does not interfere with other aspects of your life (for example drive your significant other crazy because she is always having to help bail you out when you are rushed) then we would say this style is adaptive. Reducing perfectionism about low priority items is an essential ingredient of successful time management. However, if you are working on high priority tasks item you might want to consider managing your efforts so that you can do your best work.

Knowing Yourself: The Key to Effective Time Management

Part 1: Tracking Your Time Now

The first step towards effective time management is taking the time to figure out how you currently spend your time. You may think you already know without keeping records but usually people find this phase of self-assessment most revealing. When people actually track how they spend their time they are often quite surprised to see that they are <u>not</u> spending their time the way they think are. There are, of course, exceptions. You may be one of the people who feels so controlled by time that everything is scheduled, every moment accounted for. In either case, keep a record of how you spend your time. What you schedule for the day is often not what you actually do during any particular time slot during the day. Keep track of what you actually do during each time interval and record your level of satisfaction with how you used the time.

For the satisfaction rating you can use a "+" if you were very satisfied or felt your time was spent productively. Use "0" to indicate activities that you are not satisfied with but feel are a necessary part of your schooling/job. If you are not satisfied with how you used your time mark the time slot with "-." We recommend the you use the recording sheet on the next page. Some people have a daily planner that is broken down into 15 minute units and can be used for this task as long you enter what you actually did during each interval. Keep these records for a week. The more detailed you keep your records the more you will learn about yourself.

Daily Activity Log

TIME	Description of Activity	Satisfaction Rating (--, 0, +)
5:00 am		
5:15		
5:45		
6:00		
6:15		
6:30		
6:45		
7:00		
7:15		
7:30		
7:45		
8:00		
8:15		
8:30		
8:45		
9:00		
9:15		
9:30		
9:45		
10:00		
10:15		
10:30		
10:45		
11:00		
11:15		
11:30		
11:45		
Noon		
12:15 pm		
12:30		
12:45		
1:00		
1:15		
1:30		
1:45		
2:00		
2:15		
2:30		
2:45		

3:00		
3:15 pm		
3:30		
3:45		
4:00		
4:15		
4:30		
4:45		
5:00		
5:15		
5:30		
5:45		
6:00		
6:15		
6:30		
6:45		
7:00		
7:15		
7:30		
7:45		
8:00		
8:15		
8:30		
8:45		
9:00		
9:15		
9:30		
9:45		
10:00		
10:15		
10:30		
10:45		
11:00		
11:15		
11:30		
11:45		
Midnight		
12:15 am		
12:30		
12:45		
1:00		
2:00		
3:00		
4:00		

Alan is an example of a student who is trying to improve his time management skills.

Alan is a 20-year old student majoring in Psychology. He has had problems with time management and states, "I feel like I am always rushed. I am never able to get caught up, and every time I turn around I realize I have forgotten some assignment and I end up doing a sloppy job in order to complete it on time. My performance is never as good as I know it would be if I did not procrastinate and then get rushed. I wish I could get better grades so I will be able to get into graduate school but something always seems to come up when I am just getting ready to get down to business and really hit the books."

Alan began to keep track of the events of his day. He chose to use his own paper to record his daily activities. A sample from his daily log, along with his satisfaction ratings is reproduced below.

> *Monday*
> *7:00- 7:05 Alarm goes off, get up (0)*
> *7:05-7:25 Take shower (0)*
> *7:25-7:40 Get ready, grab breakfast (a Nutria-Grain bar) as I run out the door.*
> *7:40-8:00 Drive to school, find parking spot (0)*
> *8:05-9:00 Get to class five minutes late, realize I have left my notebook for this class at home. (0)*
> *9:00-10:00 Hang around the commons, see some friends, hang with them (-)*
> *10:00-11:00 Class (+)*
> *11:00-11:15 Drive home (-)*
> *11:15-12:15 Eat lunch, watch ESPN Sportscenter (0)*
> *12:15-1:30 Try and study for my quiz in American History while watching TV, end up falling asleep (-)*
> *1:30-2:00 Drive to school, cram for my quiz. (0)*
> *2:00-3:30 Class (Get a C on quiz) (0)*
> *3:30-7:00 Drive to work at the mall, work (0)*
> *7:00-7:20 Drive home (0)*
> *7:20-9:00 Play racquetball with friend (+)*
> *9:00-11:00 Stop by girlfriend's house, eat dinner, watch TV (+)*
> *11:00- 12:00 Drive home, look over some notes (0)*
> *12:00 Go to bed. (+)*

Although Alan had good intentions in keeping his activity log he did not get as much detail regarding what exactly he was doing with his time as he would have liked. The information he has provided is a good start but more detail would have been better. Keeping track of what you do during the day using the recording sheet provided is actually easier than making one up as you go along and will give a much richer source of information when reviewing your records and establishing the different categories of activities that you engage in during a typical week. It turns out that there were a lot of "hidden" activities not detailed in Alan's activity log and so activities such work tended to get a neutral satisfaction rating of (0) when the time at work actually consisted of many different activities some satisfactory (+) and some unsatisfactory (-) in terms of whether the time was spent productively.

Nevertheless, he had a starting point and he used the information he had collected to categorize the events that consumed the most time. They were going to class, working, and watching TV. Alan was surprised at how much time he spent watching TV and how much time he spent driving to and from school. Also, he realized he was not spending nearly enough time studying. Of course, he already knew that he wasn't studying enough and he knew that he worked and that he drove back and forth to school a lot. This exercise allowed him to begin to quantify how much time he spent at these various activities so that he could better prioritize his time to spend more time doing what he wanted to do more of, namely studying.

Review Your Daily Activities. Before you proceed you will need to have completed at least five days of the daily activity log with two of the days being over the weekend. Review your sheets and sort your activities into categories of activities that best describe how you spend your time. Now you want to compare the amount of time you spend on activities that you rate as satisfactory versus unsatisfactory. Does you typical day consist of very few activities that you rate as satisfactory? This is a common occurrence for people doing this exercise for the first time because many people do not have a clear sense of what their life values are, or have concrete long term goals. Many people mostly drift. They are in college or in a particular major or particular job as much out of happenstance as from any long term planning of what they would like to do with their lives. Without a clear sense of values and goals many of our activities are simply spent "spinning our wheels."

Part 2: Values and Long-Range Goals

Not sure what you really value most in life? Try the three exercises below.

Values Exercise #1

Imagine you are in the twilight of your life and you overhear your grandchild ask your adult child "what kind of person is grandma/pa?" "What sort of things did she/he do with her/his life?" "What kind of person was she/he when she/he was your age. Write down what you hope they will say about you.

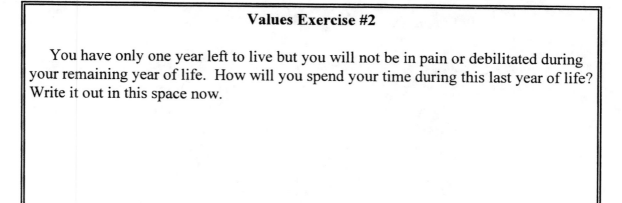

Values Exercise #2

You have only one year left to live but you will not be in pain or debilitated during your remaining year of life. How will you spend your time during this last year of life? Write it out in this space now.

Values Exercise #3

Consider what you wrote in Exercise 1 and 2 on the previous page. Now simply write your own epitaph (the brief tribute to the deceased that is written on the tomb stone).

These written exercises which you have just completed concerning your values are crucial to the success of your time management program. Without clear values it is very difficult to develop meaningful goals. <u>You need to have values to have goals</u>. You should be ready now to simply list what you value most in life (being a good friend, loving spouse and parent, social activist, accomplished pianist, successful architect, humanitarian, community leader, lover of life, sports enthusiast, etc.) whatever your personal review dictates.

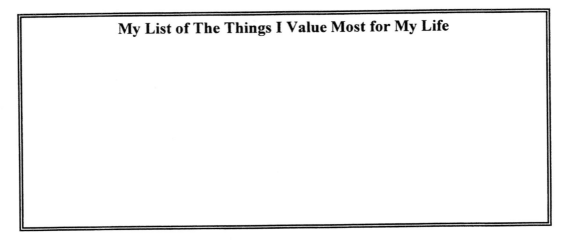

Take the time to write down the things you value the most so that you can specify what your long-range goals are. This is important because you want to plan events so that you are engaging in activities that will lead to what you consider successful living. Once you know your values, you should build long-range goals that will lead to the fulfillment of your values. For instance, if you value family, health, and money, then your long-range goals need to include these values. For instance, some common long-range goals include; getting married, have a family, getting a degree, staying healthy, finding spirituality, increase earnings, and develop a hobby. Now let's take a look at what Alan did.

Alan sat down to write out what things he most valued. He wrote: having a family, getting a good, well-paying job, and staying healthy. He then wrote out his long-term goals which included; getting married, going to graduate school, and keeping in good physical shape. His top priority short term goal is getting into graduate school and therefore he reasons he needs to make his academic work now a higher priority.

Part 3: Short-term goals

You have now taken the first two steps towards effective time management. Now you are ready to look at your goals for the upcoming week and day. At this point you may be asking, "Why am I using so much time with planning? Isn't this taking up some of my time?" Well, yes it is taking time, but if you do not have any goals you are bound to fulfill the words spoken by Benjamin Franklin, "He who aims at nothing is bound to hit it." Therefore, our long range goals and values are an essential building block towards the day-to-day development of a time schedule. If you want to have a Million Dollars in assets by the time you are 60 (not an unrealistic goal, particularly if you are just in your 20's) you need to develop long, intermediate, and short term goals to help you reach your objective. You want to set goals that are quantifiable, that you can track your progress towards achieving.

The next step is to set goals for the coming year, month and upcoming week. They should be separated into three levels. Level 1 items are those that are of the highest priority this week. For example, if there are a lot of tests scheduled in a particular week, then studying for tests would be a level 1 item. Other level 1 items may include, work, eating, sleep, writing a paper. Level 2 items are items that are activities you would like to accomplish this week, but could be put off if necessary. These may include working out, going to the movies with some friends, going on a date, calling parents. Finally, level 3 items are those items which are to be done only when all items above are completed. These may include watching TV, playing computer games, surfing the net. After these are done for the week, do the same for today. Develop level 1, 2, and 3 items for today. Now let's take a look at Alan to see his level 1, 2, and 3 items.

Alan sat down and wrote out these items for the upcoming week.

Level 1
Write mid-term paper
Study for test
Spend time with girlfriend
Go to work
Eat and sleep

Level 2
Play racquetball
Write checks for bills
Spend time with friends
Call parents, sister

Level 3
Watch TV
Play Computer Golf
Surf the Net

Alan then did the same for the next day

Level 1
Work
Eat and sleep
Read and highlight chapters 7-9 for test
Talk with girlfriend on the phone
Go to Church

Level 2
Play racquetball
Write intro for the paper

Level 3
Watch TV
Surf the Net.

Part 4: Planning Ahead

You have now reached the final part of time management, scheduling your day. You need to spend 5 minutes of a morning (or the night before) determining what your plans are for the upcoming day. Remember, if you have no plan, you will be easily distracted by level 3 items. As you plan out your day, remember to allow enough time for those activities (i.e., eating, sleeping) that are essential to life. Also, think about when you are most productive and plan to get mental activity (studying, writing) accomplished during those periods of time. Finally, as you plan your day, allow enough time to reasonably accomplish your activity. For example, if you have to drive 85 MPH to get to school or work based upon your schedule, then you need to allow more time. Now let's see what Alan did as an example.

Alan wrote out his tentative schedule for the next day
> *6:40 Get up*
> *6:40-6:50 Shower*
> *6:50-7:10 Get dressed*
> *7:10-7:30 Eat breakfast, read the sports section of the paper*
> *7:30-7:55 Drive to school, park.*
> *8:00-9:00 Class*
> *9:00-9:50 Read chapter 7*
> *10:00-11:00 Class*
> *11:00-11:45 Eat lunch I brought from home, spend time with friends*
> *11:45-1:30 Read chapters 8 & 9*
> *1:30-1:55 Do my relaxation exercises*
> *2:00- 3:30 Class*
> *3:30- 7:00 Work*
> *7:00-7:15 Drive home*
> *7:20-8:15 Play racquetball*
> *8:15-9:00 Eat dinner, call girlfriend*
> *9:00-11:30 Reread chs. 7-9, begin writing intro for paper*
> *11:30 Go to bed.*

Summary of the Four Keys to Effective Time Management	
1. Learn How You Use Your Time	Keep a diary of what you do and how much time you spend doing it
2. What are Your Values and Long-Range Goals	Answer the Questions: Long term, what do I want to be? How do I want to be remembered? What do I value? What do I Enjoy?
3. Short-Term Goals	What can you do this month, week, and day, to bring you closer to your long term goals? Establish short-term goals.
4. Planning Ahead	Plan ahead for your daily activities to insure that you engage in activities that bring you closer to your goals.

Overcoming Roadblocks

There are many things that might come up that in a day, a week, even month or year that can sidetrack a person from doing the things that they value most. You find the tips below helpful in dealing with daily drains on your time.

1. Cut down on "dead time". You might be surprised at how much time accumulates in the ten to fifteen minute intervals between activities. In a day you may have hours of "dead time." Have a book to read, do your relaxation exercises, find a place to reflect, pray, review your notes. If you want to let unscheduled time be "free" time that you can use any way you want, even "waste," give yourself permission to do so and do not feel guilty about it.

2. Allow time for plans to change. Inevitably, something in a day will not go as planned. If you have allowed extra time in a day, you will be better able to keep your schedule. If everything runs smoothly and you have a little extra time, then see #1 in overcoming roadblocks.

3. Allow yourself some personal time, and make sure you take that time. You cannot plan 24 hours a day, 7 days a week and not allow yourself some time to relax and enjoy life. You must remember that to be at your best, you cannot be burned out.

4. Learn to say "No." There are going to be people who will want to take up your time. Remember, you are in control of your time, and you must protect that fiercely, because no one else will. If you find you have a problem saying "No," then spend some time on the chapter on assertiveness training (Chapter 11) which covers in detail request refusal skills.

5. Reward yourself. Reaching your long term goals will be rewarding in their own right, but your risk not reaching them if your do not provide rewards for yourself for accomplishing smaller short term goals. Use self-praise during the day when you are doing a good job of keeping yourself focused on your goals. Provide tangible rewards for yourself for meeting daily, weekly and monthly goals. Review the consequence-based interventions discussed in Chapter 6 for ideas on how to reward yourself for making progress towards your goal in small steps.

Part Four

Stress Management

for

Specific Populations and Problems

Chapter 14

Stress Management for Head and Facial Pain

Rationale

Facial pain comes in many varieties, the most frequent being tension headache, migraine headache, and temporomandibular disorders (pain in the muscles around the "jaw joint"). Some types of facial pain are caused by organic factors such as tumors or arthritic joints. It is always prudent to have these types of organic problems ruled out by a neurologist/dental specialist and we highly recommend that you consult a physician regarding your pain, especially if the onset of pain was recent and the pain intensity has been steadily increasing. For many people with head and facial pain problems stress reactivity is one of the key contributing factors to their pain problem, although certainly not the only factor.

The figure below lists the major contributing factors associated with facial pain. The factors are ordered in terms of the extent to which they are under our control. At the bottom of the hierarchy are factors that we simply have no control over. There are a host of medical problems, including migraine headache pain and perhaps other types of head and facial pain, that have a genetic component and therefore tend to run in families. Of course, another reason headache and facial pain tend to run in families is that children often imitate their parents and adopt similar coping styles. When a parent's predominant coping style is one that tends to increase physical tension (e.g., suppressing anger, anger-in; inappropriate anger expression, anger-out,), pain problems experienced by the parent can show up later in children who adopt their parent's maladaptive coping styles. Although there have been tremendous advances in genetic engineering in recent years, it is unlikely that the genes associated with facial pain will be identified in human subjects, or prove malleable to change, among adult facial pain sufferers within our lifetime. Thus, we assume that at the time you are reading this chapter, genetic engineering will not be a viable intervention for your pain problem. Physiological reactivity is influenced by coping styles which are clearly amenable to change, as are factors such as postural influences, oral habits, and stress-reactivity. In between are factors that seem to affect head and facial pain for some people, some of the time, and that are only partially controllable.

Controllable and Uncontrollable Factors in Facial Pain

High Control	Stress Reactivity-The physiological arousal associated with stress is a prime contributor to most head and facial pain.
High Control	Posture/Oral Habits-Teeth clenching, lip biting, holding the phone with the chin, etc., all increase muscle tension which can lead to pain.
Moderate Control	Diet-Some facial pain is triggered by certain foods such as beer, chocolate, certain cheeses and wine.
Minimal Control	Allergies-Allergic responses can cause or exacerbate headache and TMD pain.
Minimal Control	Weather-some facial pain problems are influenced by barometric pressure as well as temperature.
No Control	Genetic Predispositions-some facial pain problems run in families, in part because of an inherited genetic vulnerability

The treatment of facial pain presented in this chapter is a comprehensive stress management approach aimed at changing those habits and patterns of stress reactivity that contribute to head and facial pain and that can be changed by learning new skills. The general model for stress-related facial pain suggests that stress-induced increases in physiological arousal lead to pain in the head and face. Specifically, stress reactivity leads to increased levels of tension in the muscles of the jaw, face, neck and shoulders contributing to the development of tension headache and TMD pain. Increased levels of muscle tension have also been implicated in migraine headache pain, presumably contributing to the dysregualation of the cerebral vasculature which characterizes this disorder. Postural mechanics and oral habits have been implicated as contributing factors in all three of these types of head and facial pain. Oral habits put excessive strain on the facial muscles and lead to pain. Oral habits which have been linked to the development of head and facial pain include behaviors such as clenching and grinding teeth (bruxing refers to grinding the teeth and can occur at night while you sleep or during the daytime), moving the jaw from side to side, thrusting the jaw outward, chewing gum, and repetitive chewing of other objects such as fingernails, pen caps, and pencils. The interesting feature of oral habits is that, like any other habit (pacing, knuckle cracking, even smoking), the behavior can be triggered by stress or can occur absentmindedly when there are no stressful triggers. The causal model illustrating the sequence of events in the development of facial pain is presented below.

What Causes Stress-Related Facial Pain?

Stress>>>>
leads to

Oral Habits>>>>
lead to

Muscle Hyperactivity>>>>
leads to

Facial Pain

Try This Exercise

Cup your chin in your hands so that your palms and fingers spread over your lower face from your ears to your chin. Now gently bite down on your molars. Feel the tension in the muscles in your face. Release the tension and place your finger tips on your temples. Now bite down gently on your molars and see if you can detect the tension in your temples. Continue to bite and release. Move your fingertips over your forehead, to the back of your neck at the base of your skull behind your ears, and see if you can detect changes in tension in these muscles when you bite down (do not bite too hard are too often or you will give yourself headache). The idea is to see if you can become aware of how biting (you can try other mouth movements as well) creates tension throughout the interconnected musculature of the face, neck., and shoulders. In a psychophysiology laboratory we could attach sensors to the trapezius (shoulders) and frontalis muscles (forehead) to demonstrate how muscles fairly far removed from the jaw are also activated when we use our jaw to bite, yawn, or even simply stick our tongue out.

Habit Reversal Treatment

Many facial pain sufferers knowingly or unknowingly engage in various oral habits that increase muscle tension and lead to facial pain. The intervention we describe here is designed to teach you specific skills to detect, interrupt, and reverse oral habits. As a part of the oral habit reversal treatment you will need to draw on a variety of the building block techniques presented earlier in this book. If pain is currently a major problem in your life you may have opened this book and turned immediately to this chapter. Therefore, you may not be familiar with the building block stress management skills. As the habit reversal treatment in presented in this chapter you will be referred to those chapters that teach the relevant skills needed for a successful habit reversal intervention. As these building block skills are needed, (deep breathing, relaxation training, changing maladaptive beliefs) you will need to learn or refresh your use of these techniques.

Becoming Aware of Oral Habits

By definition a habit is a behavior that can occur without your being aware of it. Therefore the key to breaking a habit is becoming aware of the habit and the situations in which the habit occurs. Once aware of a habit, you can then do something else (something incompatible with the habit) in place of the habit in order to stop the unwanted behavior. The treatment program begins by teaching exercises that increase awareness of the habit. Awareness training is facilitated by deep breathing training (Chapter 2) and progressive muscle relaxation training (PRT; Chapter 4). As you become more aware of your oral habits and the situations in which they occur, you will use specific facial exercises and deep breathing as competing responses each time you "catch" yourself in your oral habit. In this way you will be able to break your oral habits. A very similar process will be used to help you become more aware of your stress inducing thoughts and beliefs. For example, many people create stress for themselves by harboring unrealistic perfectionistic expectations for themselves and/or other people. You will learn to identify those thoughts and beliefs that cause you stress and substitute competing thoughts that are more adaptive.

Self Assessment: Facial Pain Diary and Oral Habits Diary

Facial Pain Diary. The facial pain diary is adapted from the self assessment procedures described in Chapter 3. To be able to see if the techniques you will be practicing actually influence your pain it is important to keep track of your pain levels. On the opposing pages we present an example of a pain diary that has been completed and a blank diary that you can copy for your own use. The diary is completed 4 times a day, usually on awakening, and at breakfast, lunch and dinner, in order to observe how pain levels fluctuate during the day. This is important information. People who have higher pain reports in the morning may be grinding their teeth at night. People who show an increasing trend during the day are probably showing the effects of a steady pattern of oral habits during the course of the day. Higher pain levels during the week and lower levels during the weekend suggest that specific situational stressors at work or school may need to be investigated. If you keep this diary faithfully you may want to graph your data on a weekly basis to monitor how well the intervention is working for you. Three indicators of pain frequency and intensity can be calculated from your diary. First, average pain intensity is the sum of all your ratings divided by the number of ratings (a complete diary would be the sum of the 28 entries divided by 28). A second pain measure of great importance to many pain sufferers is the highest pain rating recorded for the week. If a treatment program is working both of these values should diminish over weeks. Finally, another pain indicator of interest is number of pain free days, which should increase as you proceed through the intervention.

The diary also suggests that you record information pertaining to pain medication intake and sleep patterns. These are included in the diary because these are two collateral areas of concern for many pain patients. Specifically, you may want to monitor medication usage to see if it decreases during treatment. Some medications used to treat head and facial pain have unwanted side effects and reducing medication intake is an important goal of treatment. Also, for some people in pain, improved sleep is an important outcome of treatment. If you choose to monitor these factors, devise your own abbreviations and recording system so that weeks later when you review your diary you will remember what your entries mean.

Name_____   Week of _____

Daily Facial Pain Diary [SAMPLE]

We would like you to rate the intensity of your facial pain four times a day using the structured diary below. Please use the following scale to rate the intensity of your facial pain.

     0 = no facial pain
     1 = only aware of facial pain when attention is devoted to it
     2 = mild facial pain, could be ignored at times
     3 = facial pain is painful, but can still do my job/
          go to classes
     4 = very severe facial pain, difficult to concentrate,
          can only do undemanding tasks
     5 = intense, incapacitating facial pain

September

Date	5 Mon	6 Tue	7 Wed	8 Th	9 Fri	10 Sat	11 Sun
Awakening	3	3	2	3	4	2	2
11:00 am	A	A	A	A	T3	-	-
11:00 am	4	2	1	3	2	1	1
3:00 pm	T3	A	-	T3	A	-	-
3:00 pm	2	2	1	3	2	1	3
7:00 pm	A	A	-	A	A	-	A
7:00 pm	2	1	2	3	2	1	2
bedtime	-	-	A	A	-	-	-

<u>Meds</u>: Each time you rate your facial pain also indicate any medicine you took since the last rating. Include the name and amount of the medicine. You can make your own table of abbreviations and dosages to make filling in the chart easier.
<u>Sleep</u>: At bedtime, write down the time when you turn the lights out;
In the morning, write down how long it took to fall asleep and how many times you awoke (make a note during the night of any awakenings during the night longer than five minutes).

LEGEND - A= two Advil; T3 = 1 Tylenol#3 [make up your own recording system for Meds and Sleep]

Name_____   Week of _____

Daily Facial Pain Diary

We would like you to rate the intensity of your facial pain four times a day using the structured diary below. Please use the following scale to rate the intensity of your facial pain.

    0 = no facial pain
    1 = only aware of facial pain when attention is devoted to it
    2 = mild facial pain, could be ignored at times
    3 = facial pain is painful, but can still do my job/
        go to classes
    4 = very severe facial pain, difficult to concentrate,
        can only do undemanding tasks
    5 = intense, incapacitating facial pain

                     Month _____

Date   _____ _____ _____ _____ _____ _____ _____
             Mon   Tue   Wed   Th   Fri   Sat   Sun

Awakening
11:00 am
_____

11:00 am
3:00 pm
_____

3:00 pm
7:00 pm
_____

7:00 pm
bedtime
_____

Meds: Each time you rate your facial pain also indicate any medicine you took since the last rating. Include the name and amount of the medicine. You can make your own table of abbreviations and dosages to make filling in the chart easier.

Sleep: At bedtime, write down the time when you turn the lights out;
In the morning, write down how long it took to fall asleep and how many times you awoke (make a note during the night of any awakenings during the night longer than five minutes).

Oral Habits Diary. Typically, people are not aware of little things they do that may lead to pain until the pain is already noticeable. Different people engage in a variety of different oral behaviors that can ultimately lead to facial pain. As was noted above, the most common daytime oral habits include teeth clenching, fingernail biting, lip biting, and gum chewing. The first key to stopping these pain producing behaviors is to become aware of the habit. The second key is to figure out what the triggers are...that is, what are the situational cues associated with these habits. Most habits occur in two different types of situations: 1) absentmindedly, and 2) during stress. In general, those oral habits which occur absentmindedly can be eliminated simply by becoming aware of habit. Stress-related oral habits usually require the full habit reversal treatment to eliminate.

You will need to keep a structured diary of your oral habits similar to the one we used as an example in Chapter 3. The structured diary helps you become more aware of the thoughts and feelings associated with your oral habits and identifies the features of the situations that trigger oral habits. On the following page the sample diary is reproduced along with the key questions that you want to answer in each section of the diary. Notice that the sample diary includes both the descriptive information plus SUDS (intensity) ratings of both the intensity of the negative feelings (presented as Anxiety under the Behavior column) and intensity of Pain (presented under the Consequences column).

It would be impossible to record <u>every</u> instance of the oral habits you engage in and we do not want you to try. You do however want to record a broad range of situations and types of oral habits that you engage in. To do this you will have to become an oral habit detective. Noticing and keeping track of your oral habits should be at the very forefront of your consciousness. You need to turn up your sensitivity to your oral habits and capture as many of them on paper in your oral habits diary as practically possible.

Types of Information to Record in Your Diary

Day/Time	Antecedents	Behaviors-Actions, Thoughts, or emotions	Consequences
	When did it happen? Who were you with? What were you doing? Where were you? What thoughts and feelings were you having?	What thoughts and feelings did you have? What actions were you performing- what kind of oral habit?	What happened as a result? Was it pleasant or unpleasant?

Example Diary:

Day/Time	Antecedents	Behaviors-Actions, Thoughts or Emotions	Consequences
Monday 7:30a.m.	Driving to work, traffic is really bad, accident on the freeway	Grinding my teeth, holding tight to the steering wheel "I'm going to be late!" Feel anxious <u>Anxiety=4</u>	Felt a tightness in my jaw, pain starting in the back of my neck Ignore the pain <u>Pain=3</u>
Monday 11a.m.	Boss handed me a pile of work and said to have it done before lunch	Grinding teeth, chewing on nails, want to say something to boss but keep quiet instead <u>Anxiety=7</u>	Feel a tightness in my stomach, pain in my jaw getting worse, take 2 aspirin, <u>Pain=5</u>
Monday 7 p.m.	At home watching television	Chewing my nails thinking "why am I doing this, I don't feel stressed <u>Anxiety=1</u>	Noticed and stopped chewing <u>Pain=3</u>

Tracking Your Progress: How to Keep Good Records

1.   Make Record Keeping as Convenient as Possible. Strive for a balance between accuracy and convenience. Try to keep the best records possible without making a major stressor out of it.

2.   Develop Cues for Record Keeping. For the pain diary, for example, the easiest time to record may be when you awaken, and at lunch, dinner, and bedtime. Similarly, these may be times to review and note any situations where oral habits may have occurred since the last recording. It is important to capture some of the oral habits on paper as they occur but it is OK to make some of your recordings "after the fact" (as long as "after the fact" means hours not days). You may want to use "post-it" notes or have a significant other remind you to make records.

3.   Reinforce yourself for good record keeping through self praise and tangible rewards.

Enhancing Oral Habit Awareness Exercise

Review your oral habits diary and notice which oral habits seem to occur with greatest frequency. On a blank sheet of paper write a detailed description of the various oral habits you have noticed that you engage in. Write a separate description for each of your most prevalent oral habits. This exercise will force you to pay attention to all the sensations that are created when you clench your teeth, or bite your nails, etc. Provide as much detail as possible (e.g., how your mouth moves, what sounds are created, what the sensations feel like, etc). This type of exercise has been shown to substantially increase a person's awareness of their oral habits. Remember, you cannot begin to break a habit until you become aware of when and how the habit occurs.

Practice Progressive Muscle Relaxation Exercises

Begin regular practice of the relaxation exercises from Chapter 4 if you are not already doing so. You need to be proficient at these exercise for the oral habit reversal treatment to work well. Many pain patients are very tense generally, and specifically have a great deal of upper body tension. Regular practice of PRT exercises will lead to a reduction in baseline levels of tension and facilitate your awareness of oral habits. For some head and facial pain sufferers the deep breathing and PRT exercises alone are sufficient to bring about a dramatic decrease in pain intensity. There are several special considerations for pain patients when practicing relaxation exercises. First, it is very important that you do not tense the muscles to the point of pain in the tense and release part of the exercise. You want to tense the muscles enough to create a contrast between tension and relaxation, not cause pain. This caution is especially warranted for the jaw, chin, and neck exercise. Bite gently on your molars. A second related caution pertains to the induction of sufficient tension to produce a contrast between tension and relaxation. Some head and facial pain patients have so much upper body tension they find it difficult to notice any difference between tension and relaxation in some muscles, particularly the forehead. This is not a major problem since the limbs and other muscle groups will almost always produce noticeable contrast. Proceed through the PRT exercise and do not worry that some muscles do not get as relaxed as others, or that you have difficulty noticing the contrast in some muscles. As you practice, the contrast and relaxation that you feel in your limbs and other muscles will generalize to the more problematic muscle groups.

Deep Breathing and Facial Exercises as Competing Responses

If you have not been practicing the deep breathing exercise from Chapter 2 for a while, go back and refamliarize yourself with this exercise by practicing 3-5 times per day for several days. In addition to the deep breathing, practice tensing and releasing the three facial muscle groups covered in Chapter 4 (1. forehead, 2. eyes, nose and cheeks, 3. mouth, chin, and neck) several times per day. Initially, the practice should occur in a variety of settings and postures in order for you to become familiar with the exercises. You want to be able to perform the exercise easily whenever you choose to practice (e.g., without using the hands in the deep breathing exercise or the instruction sheet with the facial exercises). As soon as you can do these exercises easily (presumably sometime this week) then begin to use these exercises whenever you find yourself engaging in one of your oral habits. Whichever exercise you use, the end point should be the same. The phrase "lips together and teeth apart" should be your new mantra. Say this phrase to yourself every time you notice yourself engaging in one of your oral habits. Keep your jaw slack, do not allow your upper and lower teeth to touch, and let your lips rest gently together (or even slightly parted if that helps you to relax your mouth and jaw). In this position it is impossible to be clenching your teeth, biting your lip, biting the inside of your mouth, etc. Use a structured diary to track your progress.

A Review of the Steps in Oral Habit Reversal

1.   Self Assessment. Start by keeping a Pain Diary and Oral Habits Diary . You will want to keep the pain diary throughout the intervention. Two weeks of record keeping in the oral habits diary are usually required. The first week is generally spent developing a convenient recording system, developing cues to help you remember to record, and general tinkering and troubleshooting to get good records. One good week of record keeping in the structured diary will generally be sufficient though longer periods may be required, especially if the week you record is very different from most other weeks (e.g., you are on vacation, out of town on business, your kids are away at summer camp, etc.)

2.   Become Aware of Your Oral Habits. The oral habits diary will be helpful here, but in addition you need to actually write out full and graphic descriptions of your oral habits.

3.   Deep breathing and relaxation training. It is essential that you become proficient at both of these exercises. If you are motivated and practice diligently you will be ready for the next phase in 3-4 weeks. It is better to learn these exercises in order. Learn the deep breathing exercise first (Chapter 2) and then the relaxation exercise (Chapter 4).

Exercises 1, 2 and 3 can be practiced simultaneously. It is possible that you can be ready for the rest of the intervention in just 3 weeks.

4.   Interrupt the Oral Habits. Whenever you notice yourself engaging in an oral habit, stop it. If you notice you started the habit again, stop it again. Every time you notice engaging in the habit, stop it.

5.   Develop a Competing Response. When you notice and interrupt your oral habit engage in a competing motor habit that makes it difficult if not impossible to engage in your unwanted habit at the same time. The most generic competing responses are deep breathing and the facial exercise from the relaxation exercises. When you notice an oral habit, stop it, and breathe deeply and slowly, or stop and make a "clown frown." Use other competing responses that are tailored to be incompatible with your own particular oral habits. If you practice this diligently you will probably be interrupting your oral habits automatically in about two weeks.

It is not uncommon to observe dramatic pain reductions in 5-7 weeks with this intervention plan.

Other Useful Skills for Pain Management

Refuting Maladaptive Beliefs

A common thread in the previous section of this chapter was the idea that you can learn to be more aware of oral habits that increase muscle tension and use deep breathing exercises, facial muscle exercises, and progressive relaxation exercises to help break these habits. You can expand that idea and apply it to your thought patterns. You may want to learn to identify maladaptive thought patterns that lead to increased tension and substitute more adaptive thoughts. One type of thoughts to focus on are those well ingrained, general beliefs we have about ourselves and other people....specifically, the types of maladaptive beliefs discussed in Chapter 5. For example many people are chronically stressed because they set unrealistic standards for themselves and/or other people that can't possibly be met (e.g., I must be perfect, everybody must like me, life must be fair).

Select situations from the oral habits diary and identify maladaptive thoughts that may exacerbate your stress response. Several handouts from Chapter 5 including the Rational Self Help Form will facilitate both the identification of maladaptive cognitions and provide practice opportunities for refuting and changing these maladaptive beliefs. Moreover, there are some common maladaptive beliefs that are specific to pain that may also need to be challenged. Common maladaptive pain beliefs include "I can't stand this pain" and "It's not fair that I have to live with this pain." Practice refuting these types of thoughts with the self-help forms from Chapter 5.

Positive Coping Statements

After completing the exercise in refuting maladaptive beliefs, use the positive coping statement strategy presented in Chapter 10 to develop positive coping statements to use before, during, and after a stressful situation. Tailor personally relevant coping statements for each category of coping statement (i.e. Preparation, Confronting the Situation, and Reinforcing Success). Develop statements that include explicit self-directions (e.g. take three deep breaths; talk slowly and steadily) and calming statements (e.g. you're doing fine; you've gotten through this many other times in the past).

Visualization to Cope With Pain

In Chapter 7 visualization skills were presented and specific exercises for the chronic pain patient were introduced. Visualization involves using mental images to enhance relaxation as well as to compartmentalize the pain to make it more manageable. Visualization exercises are particularly useful for head and facial pain that is unremitting, as is sometimes the case after traumatic head injury. Return to Chapter 7 to review these skills and integrate visualization into your relaxation exercises.

Assertiveness Training

Many head and facial patients are interpersonally distressed. This means that a great deal of their stress is derived from interpersonal situations. Many of the pain patients we have worked with profit from the assertiveness training skills presented in Chapter 11. Review your oral habits diary and see if the situations in which you experienced the highest levels of stress were interpersonal in nature. If the answer is yes you will likely benefit from the exercises in Chapter 11 even if your pain is already substantially improved.

Teeth Grinding at Night

For some people the main cause of their pain seems to be nocturnal bruxing (nighttime teeth grinding). If your worst pain of the day is when you awaken and your jaw feels tight and sore you in all likelihood are grinding your teeth at night. An effective intervention for this source of facial pain is similar to the procedures for reversing daytime teeth clenching and other daytime oral habits. You may wonder how you can learn to be aware of your nighttime teeth grinding, more less interrupt and reverse this pain inducing habit, while you are sleeping. Its easier than you think.

You can "program" yourself to not grind your teeth while sleeping by giving yourself instructions right before you go to bed and actually practicing the sleep time habit you are trying to break. Before retiring for the night sit on the edge of the bed, take five minutes, and gently "practice" teeth grinding. Gently grate your teeth against each other and notice, in detail, what sounds you create and what sensations you experience on you teeth, gums and tongue. Do not induce pain. Practice gently and notice all the sensations you create, this will in fact increase your awareness of the habit while you sleep. Now, at the same time repeat to yourself instructions to stop the grinding while asleep. For example, say to yourself "when I feel my teeth grating against each other like this while I sleep I must stop" or "when I hear these types of sounds in my head while I sleep I must stop grinding." You might feel like that this cannot make you more aware of the habit because you will be asleep but indeed your body seems to be more aware of the habit and your preprogrammed instruction helps you to stop even when you can not remember "consciously" stopping when you awaken in the morning.

Chapter 15

Stress Management for Sexual Difficulties

Background

Most people, both men and women, have difficulty with some aspect of sexual functioning at some point in their lives. Typically these difficulties are transitory and due to situational factors. For example a woman who previously enjoyed a satisfactory orgasmic sexual relationship with one partner might experience difficulties reaching orgasm when she initiates a sexual relationship with a new partner. A man with no history of impotence might have difficulty keeping an erection following a long stressful day at work or school followed by too much alcohol in the evening. Unfortunately, transitory difficulties can become chronic problems when a person appraises these problems as being a significant threat to their self esteem and becomes excessively anxious anticipating the next sexual contact. Anticipatory anxiety may build, increasing the chances that the problem might reoccur thereby increasing anxiety further. Thus, stress is often both an antecedent and a consequence of these types of sexual problems. This "vicious cycle" sometimes leads to avoidance of sexual activities all together. When direct communication about the problem is avoided, an intimate relationship may be severely strained adding further stress and anxiety to the situation.

Sexual dysfunctions are defined as cognitive, physical or behavioral problems that prevent couples or individuals from participating in and enjoying intercourse and orgasm. Sexual variations or unconventional sexual behavior are not considered to be sexual dysfunctions as long as the participants freely consent, are of legal age, and enjoy the sexual contact. Only if the unconventional sexual behavior leads to guilt or anxiety in the participants which diminishes sexual enjoyment and negatively affects performance would treatment be warranted. Both heterosexuals and homosexuals may experience sexual dysfunctions. Since the physiological mechanisms of arousal and orgasm are universal regardless of sexual orientation, we hope that all individuals who read this chapter may find it helpful. This chapter focuses primarily on those types of sexual difficulties in which anxiety and stress play a major role. Specifically, the chapter focuses on male erectile problems and female orgasmic difficulties. Painful intercourse accounts for some female orgasmic difficulties and therefore a section of the chapter presents an intervention specifically for this problem.

Sexual Dysfunction in Men: Erection Problems

Erection problems are the most frequent sexual problems experienced by men. Erectile failure is the inability of a male to achieve or maintain an erection. This can be due to either physical problems or psychological issues or a combination of the two. About 35% of all erectile function problems are due to physical factors. Nighttime erections are a characteristic feature of sleep. If a man has an erection while sleeping, a physical problem probably does not account for the difficulty in having an erection during sex. A thorough evaluation by a urologist is an important step in evaluating the cause of erectile problems. In addition to a physical examination there are a number of tests that the urologist might order to assess the nature of the problem. These tests may range from an overnight evaluation in a sleep laboratory to a simple home test where the man fastens a small strap around the penis which pops open during sleep if an erection occurs. In the box which follows you will find a "do-it-yourself" procedure for assessing whether erectile difficulties are due to physiological or emotional/behavioral processes.

Erectile Problems: Physical or Psychological?
A Do-it-Yourself Home Test

Buy a roll of stamps. Tear off as many stamps as is necessary and wrap a band of stamps around the base of the penis (contrary to popular mythology, how many stamps you need does not predict the outcome of the test). Go to sleep. When you wake up in the morning check the perforations between the stamps. If the penis becomes erect during the night, the perforations between the stamps will tear or break and chances are the erectile problem is due to emotional/behavioral processes. However, if no tearing in the perforations between the stamps has occurred after one or two nights, a medical problem is suggested and a physical exam is recommended.

If the perforations are broken, or if you know without trying the do-it-yourself test that your problems are mostly related to situational cues in your environment, be grateful. Yes, be grateful. The cognitive behavioral interventions developed for these types of problems are highly efficacious and far less invasive (literally) than many of the medical interventions available.

Techniques to Correct Erectile Difficulties and Premature Ejaculation

Premature ejaculation refers to ejaculation that occurs before the individual wants it to occur during sexual activity. What constitutes a problem with premature ejaculation is very subjective. Previous attempts to define premature ejaculation quantitatively, such as ejaculation that occurs with eight or less pelvis thrust, or ejaculation that occurs in less than one minute following penetration, have proved unsatisfactory. It should be noted that unrealistic beliefs sometimes contribute to the problems that are labeled "premature ejaculation." For example, a man (or his partner) who complains that "he cannot last more than 20 minutes" has unrealistic beliefs about how long he should be able to delay ejaculation in order to please his partner. The average length of time between penetration and ejaculation is less than three minutes. Clearly the distinction between a premature ejaculation problem in the man and an orgasmic dysfunction in the woman is fuzzy. A point which we will emphasize later is that most of the "problems" discussed in this chapter are a couple's problem. The idea is not to identify the partner who has a "Problem" but rather to take responsibility as a couple for enhancing the intimacy and pleasure of both partners without "playing the blame game."

The sensate focus exercises described later in this chapter are a good place to start for a couple in the fuzzy area between a man who ejaculates more quickly than both partners would like and a woman who takes much longer to orgasm than both partners would like. Performance anxiety is the primary contributor to both problems and the sensate focus exercises are designed to take the performance aspect out of sexual intimacy and emphasize pleasurable stimulation that is not goal directed. In addition to the sensate focus exercises a man who wants to increase ejaculatory control might want to use the squeeze technique. This is a very simple, but extremely effective technique to increase ejaculatory control.

Squeeze Technique. A Man can practice this technique by himself or with his partner in order to learn to better control the timing of ejaculation. Either by yourself or with a partner stimulate the penis to the point just before you feel you are about to ejaculate. Then squeeze the penis firmly for about 15 seconds by placing the thumb and index fingers firmly on the upper shaft of the penis just beneath the penis head. Relax the muscles in your legs and buttocks. The penis will lose some of its erection. Wait half a minute or so and then stimulate the penis again just before ejaculation and use the squeeze technique again. Repeat the process four or five times. Do this for several sessions over the next week or two. You will be amazed at how much control over ejaculation that this simple exercise provides.

Erectile Difficulties. For many men, difficulties with getting and maintaining an erection is a problem that develops subsequent to problems with premature ejaculation. Anxiety about ejaculating prematurely generalizes to anxiety about one's ability to perform sexually in general, and erectile difficulties ensue. Just as frequently, erectile difficulties develop simply from performance anxiety without a history of premature ejaculation. Regardless of the origins of the problem (assuming an organic problem is not the cause) the treatment is the same. Wolpe developed a systematic desensitization treatment in the 1950s and Masters and Johnson developed a variation in the 1970s that has been adopted by many in the field of sex therapy. The cornerstone of the Masters and Johnson approach is sensate focus exercises. Later in this chapter the sensate focus exercises are described in detail and these exercises are often all that is needed to resolve problems experienced by both men and women with sexual difficulties. Men with erectile difficulties may want to add a variation of the squeeze technique described in stage 4 of the sensate focus exercises.

Sexual Dysfunction in Women: Orgasmic Dysfunction and Painful Intercourse

Difficulty reaching an orgasm and painful intercourse are the most frequent sexual problems experienced by women. Orgasmic dysfunction is often categorized into primary and secondary orgasmic dysfunction. In primary orgasmic dysfunction, a woman has never had an orgasm through any type of sexual stimulation. It has been estimated that about 15% of women who seek treatment for sexual dysfunction problems suffer from primary orgasmic dysfunction. In secondary orgasmic dysfunction, which is far more prevalent, a woman has achieved orgasm at some point in time but is unable to orgasm at the present time, or is only able to do so very infrequently, or is unable to orgasm under her preferred conditions (e.g., can masturbate to orgasm but prefers orgasm during intercourse).

Dyspareunia refers to painful intercourse. The pain in dyspareunia can range from vaginal irritation to severe pain during intercourse. Vaginismus is painful intercourse associated with a specific muscular reflex. Here the muscles in the lower third of the vagina close tightly during attempted intercourse thereby preventing penetration. This is an involuntary muscle contraction thought to be acquired via classical conditioning. Painful intercourse may occur on one occasion due to any number of physical conditions (insufficient vaginal lubrication, vaginal irritation, etc). As a defensive response these muscles contract to prevent further injury or damage. On subsequent occasions the cues associated with intercourse act as conditioned stimuli which elicit the reflexive muscle contraction.

Factors Influencing the Development of Sexual Dysfunctions

Some of the most common factors that contribute to the development of sexual dysfunctions are listed in the table presented on the following page. These elements may all affect a person's sexual performance and enjoyment, either singly or in combination. They interact with each other as well, sometimes compounding the problem in a "vicious cycle" of escalating dysfunction. With so many factors involved you may wonder why more people don't have problems! The truth is, lots of people do have sexual dysfunction problems. You may not hear about it largely because people are often embarrassed to discuss sexual problems. On the bright side, there is a lot a person can do to improve his or her sex life if a problem does occur.

Factors Contributing to Sexual Dysfunctions

Physical and Physiological factors
        examples: illness, surgery, medication, reaction to contraceptives

Previous Environmental Problems
        examples: rape, incest, extreme religious upbringing

Misinformation and/or a Lack of Knowledge Regarding Sex
        This was probably a greater problem in the past when sex was not so readily
        displayed in the media. However, one still needs to have a basic knowledge of
        what parts of the body are involved, and how they normally react. Sometimes,
        simple education can go a long way to improve performance and enjoyment.

Personal Lack of Skill or Lack of Skill in a Partner
        This has components similar components to a lack of knowledge, but also may
        include a lack of communication between partners. People not only need to
        know what feels good to them and what they enjoy, but they must also be able
        to communicate these preferences to their partner, and listen to what their
        partner prefers as well.

Psychological Factors
        examples: anxiety, depression, strong religious beliefs, maladaptive beliefs

Other Problems in the Relationship
        examples: marital conflict, anger and hostility, lack of trust, lack of attraction,
        general lack of communication

Self Assessment: Identifying Maladaptive Beliefs

Of course, before you can plan an intervention you need to gather some information about yourself. It is clear that you will not want to pull out a structured diary and record information while you are engaging in sexual activity. You can, however, analyze the situation after the fact to better understand the pattern of thoughts and feelings that are likely contributing to the problem. In particular, an individual's beliefs about how they "should" respond and "ought" to perform often produce increased anxiety associated with these types of male and female sexual problems. The most important thing for you to identify (and refute) are the maladaptive beliefs you hold about the situation which increase your anxiety. Use the Thoughts Diary from Chapter 5 to track both your emotions and cognitions regarding your sexual difficulties. You want to make an entry whenever you experience negative emotions related to your sexual difficulties. Keep your diary for about a week and then look for patterns in your ways of thinking and responding emotionally. Note all of the different irrational beliefs listed on page __ that your patterns of thinking fit under. As you proceed with the direct action interventions presented in this chapter, develop on your own intervention for your maladaptive, irrational beliefs using the self-help form on page ___ and other information in chapter 5.

While you are keeping your thoughts diary, it is important to keep in mind that sexual problems do not occur in a vacuum. In addition to stress and anxiety, any concerns that surface such as marital problems, substance abuse, lack of knowledge, lack of communication, lack of intimacy, or physical factors, will need to be addressed as well. And since many of the sexual dysfunctions presume sexual intercourse with a partner, it is important to remember that sexual dysfunctions, regardless of who displays them, are the responsibility of both partners. Regardless of the original cause of the dysfunction, both partners are often responsible for the maintenance of the problem. Therefore, it is especially important to elicit your partner's help and support in the solution.

Treatment

The theory behind the development of sexual dysfunctions has changed dramatically over the years. Starting in the early 1900s through the first half of the twentieth century, sexual dysfunctions were thought to be caused by deep-seated personality conflicts developed during childhood resulting from improper maturation through Freud's stages of psychosexual development. As a result, sexual dysfunctions were treated with intensive psychotherapy. It was not until Masters and Johnson published Human Sexual Inadequacy in 1970 that an alternate therapeutic approach became popular. Masters and Johnson took a cognitive behavioral approach to counseling couples with the goal being the removal of symptoms as opposed to uncovering the unconscious conflict through psychotherapy.

Sensate Focus

Sensate focus has been the cornerstone of sex therapy since Masters and Johnson first introduced the procedure in 1970. Sensate focus emphasizes a heightened awareness of, and focus on, the pleasurable sensations associated with sexual activity. The idea is to teach people to learn to pay attention to the *process* of sexual intimacy (pleasurable sensations of touch, taste and smell) and not the outcomes (erection, orgasm). Sensate focus procedures give you "permission" to ignore performance concerns ("will I be able to stay hard?," "If I don't come soon he is going to get frustrated and give up").   Freedom from these performance concerns is achieved by initially restricting the types of sexual activity you and your partner engage in to only those activities not involving intercourse. Knowing in advance that intercourse will not be an outcome frees you and your partner to explore multiple avenues of pleasure without a background concern of "what is this foreplay going to lead too?" The exercises will lead to enhanced awareness of sexual pleasures that do not involve intercourse per se. These exercises also serve to open channels of communication between you and your partner so that you may learn and teach each other what each of you finds pleasurable. To further enhance your communication patterns with your partner you may want to refer to the section on communication skills training in Chapter 12 and the "making requests" section of Chapter 11.

Sensate Focus Exercises

1. Touching Exercises. The first step in sensate focus involves exercises where you and your partner touch, caress, and fondle each other everywhere but the breast (female) and genital area. You want to have fun exploring and pleasuring each other's body. Massage and caress each other with different strokes. Try deep massage and light fingertip caress and everything in between. Experiment with different types of touch and enjoy the sensations associated with both giving and receiving pleasure. Gently communicate with each other how the different types of touch make you feel. Take turns being the giver and receiver of pleasurable touch. Try receiving touch while lying on your stomach with your partner straddling you and also while lying flat on your back. Take a turn at giving pleasurable touch in these same positions. Try sitting face to face, legs entwined, and touch, massage, and caress each others face, arms and hands. Find the unexpected sites of pleasure. Perhaps a light touch in the crook of the arm or knee, a hand massage, a finger trace of the face. Experiment and focus your attention on the pleasant sensations this exercise creates. You may want to begin these exercises with your clothes on for the first several sessions before trying them with your clothes removed.

2. Genital Pleasuring. Continue with the touching exercises and extend them to include the breasts and genital area. As you include genital pleasuring in your touching exercises do not exclude the rest of the body. Use the same sense of experimentation to your exploration of genital pleasuring as you did in the body touching exercises. Try different strokes, different amounts of pressure, be playful and gentle. Stimulation of the female genitals might begin with a gentle finger trace of the outside of the vagina. Gentle touching of the clitoris can proceed once the woman is aroused. Similarly, do not insert fingers into the vagina until the woman is aroused. If there is anxiety at this step go slower and use less direct genital stimulation. For example run the fingers through the pubic hair, squeeze and gently pull the buttocks, lightly brush the inner thighs and abdomen. Do not proceed with more direct contact until your partner can enjoy this phase without anxiety. Talk to each other to find the right pace. Similarly, a slow and gentle pace when initially stimulating the male genital seems to work best. Stroke the scrotum, the inside of the thighs, and the abdomen. Caress the penis. Intensify the stimulation with vigorous stroking of the penis from the base of the penis and up the shaft of the penis and let your partner communicate what feel good. Let your partner's arousal wax and wane by moving from the genitals to pleasuring other parts of the body. Throughout this both of you want to focus on the pleasant sensations of arousal. There is no pressure to perform, these exercises are not going to lead to intercourse. You want to give and receive and pleasure and focus on pleasurable sensations created by your body. Focus on and enjoy the sensations as your partner strokes and caresses you. Take turns pleasuring each other and try pleasuring each other at the same time.

3. Genital Pleasuring with Vaginal Containment. During a session of genital pleasuring, when both partners are relaxed and aroused you want to add an exercise termed vaginal containment. The idea is for the woman to insert her partner's penis into her vagina and simply hold or "contain" the penis in her vagina. It doesn't matter if the penis is hard or completely flaccid, the woman can still gently insert the penis into her vagina. You and your partner want to keep a sense of humor as well as a sense of exploration for this exercise since initially it might seem a bit awkward. With the man lying comfortably on his back the woman can straddle him at the hips, resting on her knees and facing her partner. If her knees are about even with his nipples the genital areas will be aligned making it easier to insert the penis. The woman then gently guides the penis into the vagina. This process allows the woman to control penetration, which is important if vaginismus has been a problem. Another advantage is that it allows the man to completely relax and enjoy the sensations without worrying about having an erection or other "performance" issues. It will probably take several tries the first time you do this exercise, but keep trying, talk to each other, and keep a sense of humor. Once the penis is in the vagina remain still and focus on the sensations. The woman can then contract her vaginal muscles (same muscle movement used when stopping the flow of urine mid stream.) rhythmically as both partners enjoy the pleasant sensations. This can continue for a few seconds or several minutes. In this phase, practice two or three vaginal containment exercises each genital pleasuring session.

4. Intercourse. Once the genital pleasuring with vaginal containment exercise becomes easy and natural, begin adding movement to the exercise. It is typically recommended that the woman initiate movement first, taking note of what movements increase sexual pleasure. Partners can then take turns moving. Initially, keep the movements slow and easy. After several sessions introduce more rapid and vigorous movements. At this point you are ready for full sexual intercourse. It is important to note that intercourse is not synonymous with orgasm. The focus remains on increasing mutual pleasure not on performance outcomes. The majority of women do not experience orgasm without clitoral stimulation. You may want to add this to intercourse with either the man or woman stimulating the clitoris during thrusting, or with the use of a vibrator. Just as frequently couples take turns pleasuring each other to orgasm through intercourse, genital pleasuring, and oral sex. Intercourse is not the only way to achieve an orgasm, and with women, it is not the most frequent method.

General Guidelines for Sensate Focus

1. One of the essential features of sensate focus is to refrain from sexual intercourse during the early phases (at least the first two) of the program. Agree to this before you start, then no matter how aroused one or both of you may become, you know that the arousal is not going to be followed by intercourse and you can relax and simply enjoy the pleasuring. By "prohibiting" sexual intercourse you remove all the performance demands that are associated with orgasmic and erectile function problems.

2. It is OK to release sexual tension that is generated by these exercises by masturbation. In the first phase, however, if you want to masturbate, do so in private away from your partner. In the later stages of genital pleasuring you may want to stimulate each other to orgasm by mutual masturbation but it will depend on the couple and the types of sexual problems you have been having. If the man has had erectile problems, stimulation to orgasm at this point may be desirable. A woman with difficulties reaching orgasm may find introducing the possibility of mutual masturbation to orgasm too threatening at this point. Its a couple's decision. Talk to each other. If things do not work out the way you would like, drop back a step in the program for a while.

3. There is a great deal of variability in how rapidly couples progress through these stages and some couples choose to enjoy step one and step two activities exclusively. It is not a race. Two weeks at each stage with three sessions a week is a general guideline. One week at each stage is probably the minimum.

Anxiety

As is clear by now anxiety is often a primary contributor to sexual dysfunctions. Anxiety and stress can affect sexual enjoyment and performance in two ways. First, it may prevent the individual from focusing on the pleasurable physical sensations that are a part of sexual arousal and instead lead the individual to focus too much on achieving "goals" such as an erection, orgasm, or ejaculation. In other words, this is one activity where it is possible for a person to try too hard! As was the case in the sensate focus exercises, often, just freeing yourself of the responsibility to perform increases enjoyment and makes it less likely that you will encounter any problems.

Second, there is a physiological reason why anxiety and stress increase the probability of sexual dysfunctions. Anxiety and stress activate the sympathetic nervous system. In the companion text to this workbook you learned that, the sympathetic nervous system and the parasympathetic nervous system work in a reciprocal fashion. In other words, they are physiologically incompatible. They cannot both be dominant at the same time. In general, sexual arousal is a parasympathetic nervous system activity and orgasm a sympathetic activity. Therefore, performance anxiety, by activating the sympathetic nervous system precludes the activation of the parasympathetic functions necessary for sexual arousal. Often the gradual introduction of anxiety provoking situations in the sensate focus exercise allows the anticipatory anxiety to extinguish. Sometimes, however, anxiety prevents a person from attempting the sensate focus exercises and a more structured intervention aimed directly at the anxiety is needed. Systematic desensitization has proved to be extremely effective in such cases.

Systematic Desensitization

Systematic desensitization is a common component of successful sex therapy where stress or anxiety is a large component of the problem, regardless of whether the anxiety is the cause of the dysfunction or a result of it. Systematic desensitization was described in the companion text as a structured program where, during a state of relaxation, an individual is exposed via imagery to situations that elicit ever increasing levels of anxiety. At each level, the individual is taught to relax until the situation no longer causes anxiety. The principle of reciprocal inhibition indicates that a person cannot be both relaxed and anxious at the same time (the sympathetic nervous system and parasympathetic nervous system can not both be dominant at the same time). Therefore, if you gradually introduce anxiety provoking imagery while remaining relaxed the anxiety will diminish. Moreover, there is evidence that simply exposing an individual to increasingly more anxiety provoking situations results in decreased anxiety presumably in part because the person is learning about their ability to cope in the process. There are five main steps in systematic desensitization as used in the sex therapy literature.

1. Deep Breathing and Relaxation Exercises

At this point in the workbook you are probably already skilled at deep breathing and progressive muscle relaxation exercises presented in Chapters 2 and 4, respectively. If however you turned to the current chapter and want to try the systematic desensitization exercise you will need to go back and practice the exercises in Chapters 2 and 4.

2. Anxiety Hierarchy

You will need to build an anxiety hierarchy similar to the stressful events hierarchy discussed in Chapter 12. Please review this section of Chapter 12 now so you will be able to create your own stressful events hierarchy for the anxiety associated with your sexual difficulties. Basically you will want to generate a list of 16-20 anxiety producing situations or events related to your sexual difficulties. Below are a few sample items and their SUDS ratings from a review (LoPiccolo & Lobitz, 1978) of the use of systematic desensitization for women who report negative or aversive emotional reactions to intercourse.

Anxiety Hierarchy

Description of the Situation	SUDS
1. You are dancing with your boyfriend/husband fully clothed	15.9
2. He kisses you in a warm suggestive way on the lips	27.8
3. You caress you partners' genitals while you are clothed	38.5
4. He caresses your genital area while clothed	50.3
5. He inserts his finger into your vagina during foreplay	59.7

Since each individual's situation and concerns are unique, the hierarchy that you create will be personalized just for you.

3. Imagined Rehearsal

Imagined rehearsal is outlined in detail in the chapter on Stress Inoculation. Basically you want to begin with progressive muscle relaxation training. Once relaxed you want to vividly imagine the scene lowest on your anxiety hierarchy. If you start to get anxious, quit the scene and return to the relaxation exercises. Repeat this process until you can imagine the scene in vivid detail and remain relaxed. You proceed up the hierarchy in the same manner until the most anxiety provoking situation on your hierarchy can be imagined while remaining relaxed.

4. Abstaining From Sex.
It is important to abstain from all sexual activity that produces anxiety, while you are going through the systematic desensitization procedure. Do not put yourself in a situation listed on your anxiety hierarchy until you have gone through the steps of imagining yourself and relaxing in each stressful situation.

5. Sensate Focus.
Once you have been able to go through the entire hierarchy without becoming anxious, then it is time to practice these situations in real life. Use the sensate focus exercises to help move you through your hierarchy in real life. Of course it will be important for your partner to understand, support, and cooperate with your efforts throughout this process.

Everyone Can Have an Orgasm (but maybe not at the same time)

Women who have never have had an orgasm can learn to do so through self-exploration and masturbation and then combine these techniques with sensate focus activities with a partner to enjoy a mutually satisfying sexual relationship. The exercises which follow are adapted from a procedure LoPiccolo and colleagues developed in the early 1970's, and which have been used by countless sex therapists since when working with women whose primary complaint is never having had an orgasm. It is much easier for women to orgasm through manual stimulation of the genitals than through intercourse. These exercises allow you to learn what brings you pleasure so that you can bring yourself to orgasm. If you have a supportive partner you can then use the sensate focus exercises to teach your partner what pleases you. These exercises are effective for a number of reasons. The most obvious advantage of these exercises is that a person does not need a partner to practice them. Moreover, by practicing these exercises alone you can focus completely on yourself without any worry about what a partner might be thinking or what you "should" be doing for a partner. Finally, these exercises are similar to the graded exposure techniques you learned about in the companion text. That is, you will move from step to step only after you practice the exercises in a given step and do not feel anxious. A standard six step hierarchy, with exercises for each step is described below.

Six Steps to Becoming Orgasmic

1. Increase Physical Self-Awareness

Many women who are not orgasmic find that they feel anxious when looking at or touching their genitals or sometimes even looking at pictures of female genitals. We considered including pictures here to help with this problem but it turned out that genitals do not look right on stick figures (which is the highest level of our combined artistic ability). Fortunately, the exercises works best if you look at your own genitals anyway. Find a private area, remove all clothing, and visually examine your body. Use a hand mirror to visually explore the genital area. During this step, concentrate on the physical nature and beauty of your body. You may feel uneasy doing this exercise. You want to continue practicing it until you do not feel uneasy looking at your genitals. Most people who are uneasy with this exercise have maladaptive beliefs about their body in general and masturbation and sex in particular. The procedures in Chapter five will help you identify and change the maladaptive beliefs that contribute to your anxiety.

2. Genital Exploration

Continue with step one and begin to explore your body through touch in addition to the visual process above. The purpose of this step is to become comfortable with the sight and feel of your genitals. Since this exercise is practiced alone, it also removes any evaluation anxiety.

3. Locate Sensitive Areas

Now elaborate on the previous step by concentrating on the sensations that you create while physically exploring your body and genitals. The goal in this step is to find those areas that produce the most pleasure.

4. Manually Stimulate Pleasurable Areas

Now that you know which areas feel pleasurable when stimulated, concentrate on manually stimulating those areas. Try various techniques for stimulation including differing amounts of pressure and lubrication to see what feels best.

5. Increase Intensity and Duration of Pleasurable Stimulation

Now increase the intensity and duration of the pleasurable stimulation. Continue to manually stimulate yourself and let the sensation of pleasure build until orgasm occurs. This could happen very rapidly or it may take forty-five minutes or longer at one time before orgasm occurs. You may reach a plateau stage where the stimulation is extremely pleasurable but doesn't reach that final stage of orgasmic inevitability. Relax and enjoy the pleasant sensations. Focus on the process, the feelings of pleasure now, not the goal of orgasm. If you start to get tired or sore stop the exercise and practice again on another day.

6. Enhancing Masturbation

If you have practiced the exercises in step 5 across several different practice sessions without orgasm you should purchase a vibrator. A round headed body massager is preferable to a phallic shaped vibrator. Continue with the exercises in step 5 using the vibrator to provide stimulation. Experiment with the vibrator. You may apply it directly to sensitive parts of the genitals or indirectly, such as by placing it over the fingers. Read erotic literature, use fantasy and develop visually arousing images to enhance your excitement. You almost certainly will reach orgasm in this stage.

Overcoming Roadblocks

If you tried the procedures outlined in this chapter but did not obtain the results you desired there are several possible roadblocks but two that predominate.

1. The anxiety that accompanies most of the problems discussed in this book may persist despite your best efforts to use the various anxiety management techniques described.

2. Another common roadblock is that you have tried to work with your partner but have found barriers in your communication patterns that prevent the two of you from trying some of these techniques.

3. As noted earlier in the chapter it is possible that your difficulties are related in part to physical factors. You may be taking medication that interferes with sexual processes. Similarly, certain medical conditions, such as some cases of diabetes, interfere with sexual functioning. Recreational drug use, particularly alcohol, as well as fatigue and stress can diminish sexual pleasure.

If these or other roadblocks describe your situation you may want to consider seeking help from a certified sex therapist. You can look in your yellow pages under Psychologists or Marriage Counselors to find someone in your area that provides services in sex therapy. In addition, the American Association of Sex Educators, Counselors, and Therapists will provide a list of certified sex therapists in your area if you send two dollars and a self-addressed envelope to:

American Association of Sex Educators, Counselors, and Therapists
435 N. Michigan Ave
Suite 1717
Chicago, Il 60611-4067

When you call a potential therapist ask about the services they provide, the type of training they have had, how much experience they have. If you think you should not, or could not do this because its too embarrassing or aggressive, go back to Chapter 5 and identify the maladaptive beliefs that leads to this emotional consequence. My advice is that if a therapist or the therapist's staff can not help you feel at ease when you ask these types of questions you probably do not want to see that person for sex therapy.

Chapter 16

Stress Management and Substance Abuse: Smoking Cessation and Controlled Drinking

Background

Many people self-medicate (take sedative drugs) as a way to manage their anxiety. The text book which accompanies this workbook describes the drugs of use and abuse in stress management, both legal and illegal, as well as the various anxiety disorders in which substance abuse is a collateral feature. However, one of the drugs most associated with stress, nicotine, is not a sedative drug in the classic sense of the word. Nicotine produces paradoxical effects in that it acts as a stimulant (acts as both a central nervous system stimulant and stimulates most directly the sympathetic division of the autonomic nervous system) but it also stimulates the sensory fibers in your muscles making them feel more relaxed. Depending on the situation, it is not uncommon for the same person to report that they smoked for a "pick-me-up" and to help them relax both in the same day. The relaxing effects of smoking during stress, however, seems to be one of the crucial factors that maintains smoking behavior. People who stop smoking, but then relapse, report that stress is the number one trigger for returning to smoking.

Alcohol of course is also a drug frequently used and abused by people trying to manage their stress and anxiety, and it is not uncommon for people to drink and smoke in the same setting. There are important differences in the pattern of use of these two drugs and the effects of withdrawal. Smoking and excessive alcohol use have increasingly become stigmatized behaviors in the United States. Many people want to alter their pattern of consumption of one or both of these substances both for their health and to conform to the pressures placed on them by others in their environment. The vast majority of adult smokers report that they wish they did not smoke. They recognize the health risks of smoking and report that it is a bad habit. Those seeking to change their smoking behavior generally strive to quit as opposed to just cut down. Alcohol consumption has a different pattern in that most people's definition of a "problem drinker" is someone who drinks more than they do. You may want to change your drinking behavior in certain situations but not give up alcohol altogether. Whereas health concerns and social stigma motivate most people seeking to quit smoking, it is the consequences of drinking that typically motivates people to change their pattern of drinking. For example, if you get anxious when you study and calm your nerves with a beer but fall asleep, never get around to studying, and do poorly on tests you may be motivated to change your pattern of drinking behavior but not necessarily quit altogether.

This chapter will be helpful for the person who wants to quit smoking or reduce their intake of alcohol. A smoking cessation program is provided in detail. The controlled drinking section draws on these same techniques and procedures and encourages you to build an intervention that is suited to your particular problem situations. If you are a heavy drinker and want to quit you should consult your physician. Alcohol withdrawal in the person who is physiologically dependent can be life threatening. This workbook is designed for the person who is a mild to moderate drinker who wants to learn to exert better control over his or her drinking behavior.

Overview of Smoking Cessation Procedures

The stop smoking plan outlined in subsequent sections draws from our own clinical practice as well as the research and clinical applications of Ovide Pomerleau, Alan Marlatt, the smoking cessation literature provided by the American Lung Association and the educational materials provided by marketers of nicotine replacement therapy (nicotine gum and nicotine patch). You may be familiar with the gloomy statistic that only 15% of the attempts to quit smoking are successful. The picture is not as dark as this statistic may suggest however. Of those who have successfully quit smoking (been a non smoker for more than a year), it took an average of 7 quit attempts before they were successful. These statistics tell us that eventually most people who want to quit smoking are successful. Therefore you want to develop a stop smoking program with optimism and include features that will maximize your chance of success.

There is no "best" way to quit. Some people prefer a fading technique where they gradually reduce their consumption while others prefer to "stop cold turkey." Use the questions in the box on the following page to help you decide which method is best for you. The procedures described in this workbook include a plan for gradual reduction of cigarette consumption over a four week period followed by techniques to assist you once you reach "quit day" and beyond. We encourage you to seriously consider following the plan outlined here but if you are determined to quit "cold turkey" you will find the suggestions and tips in the section Quit Day and Beyond very helpful. Nicotine replacement therapy has been shown to almost double your chance of successfully quitting smoking. The information box on the following page describing nicotine replacement therapy may help you decide whether to include nicotine replacement therapy in your intervention plan.

Choosing a Quit Method

Answer the following questions to determine which method is best for you.

1. Have you ever quit "cold turkey" and stayed off cigarettes for at least one week? **YES** _____ **NO** _____

2. Have you ever gradually reduced the number of cigarettes you smoked and then stayed off cigarettes for at least one week? YES____ NO_____

3. Do you Currently smoke one and half or more packs of cigarettes per day? YES____ NO____

If you answered "YES" to either 1 or 2, choose that method again, since it worked for you before.

If you answered "YES" to both 1 and 2, look at your answer to question 3. If you smoke less than one and a half packs a day and have previously quit cold turkey, choose that approach again. If you smoke more than one and a half packs per day and have previously quit by tapering, choose that approach.

If you have unsuccessfully tried either method before, try the other one this time.

If you have never tried to quit before, or if you are still undecided, use gradual reduction (tapering) if you smoke one and a half or more packs a day. Use "cold turkey" if you smoke less than one and half packs per day.

146

Nicotine Replacement Therapy

Nicotine replacement therapy has been shown to almost double your chances of success at smoking cessation. The basic idea behind nicotine replacement therapy is to provide the person with a measured dose of nicotine (absent of all the tar and other carcinogens found in cigarettes) to ease the cravings associated with nicotine withdraw. The nicotine literally serves as a replacement for the nicotine otherwise obtained by smoking and makes the initial weeks of smoking cessation less difficult. Use of nicotine replacement therapy is gradually reduced as you break the associations between cues in your environment and smoking.

Once you get to your quit day you should consider including it in your treatment plan (though if you find it objectionable, be reassured that thousands have successfully quit smoking without nicotine replacement therapy). You should never use nicotine replacement therapy while you are still smoking. If you choose to use nicotine replacement therapy, wait until your quit day to begin using it.

Nicotine replacement therapy comes in two forms; the nicotine patch and nicotine gum. Both are now available without a prescription. Nicotine gum was introduced first as an adjunct to smoking cessation but its popularity waned somewhat following introduction of the nicotine patch (also called the transdermal system since absorption is through the skin). Initially, most people found the nicotine gum unpleasant in taste and texture but these qualities have been improved upon in recent years. You must decide which nicotine delivery system is best for you. Nicotine gum is an attractive choice for some people because there is an increased sense of control in deciding whether to chew or not. There are also anecdotal reports that the weight gain associated with smoking cessation is less with nicotine gum relative to the patch (perhaps because eating and chewing the gum are incompatible with each other). The advantage of the patch on the other hand is that you put it on in the morning and forget about it for the rest of the day. The patch assures a constant level of nicotine in your system.

The decision of whether to use nicotine replacement therapy of course is yours. Success rates with nicotine gum and the patch are about equal and your choice should simply be one of personal preference. Your primary care physician can give you more information about nicotine replacement therapy.

We suggest a four-week plan whereby you gradually gain control over your urge to smoke. The four-week plan is designed to promote rapid progress towards your goal of total abstinence. As you gradually smoke less and less you will be learning to change your smoking habits and you will be able to practice these new behaviors in the easiest situations first and tackle more difficult situations as your skill level and confidence increases. Analyzing the situations in which you smoke is the first step in the program and not surprisingly a situational analysis begins with self assessment.

Self Assessment

Smoking is a both a habit and an addiction. Situational cues and physiological cues both influence your smoking behavior. It is important to obtain a careful record of the cigarettes you smoke, and the situations in which you smoke, in order to determine the triggers for your habit. Smoking is sometimes triggered by strong physiological sensations of craving. By terminating the unpleasant sensations associated with cravings smoking behavior is negatively reinforced. That is, smoking behavior is maintained because the behavior terminates an unpleasant stimulus. On the other hand when you smoke in certain situations where you associate smoking with increased pleasure the behavior is positively reinforced. For example, many people find the cigarette they have after sex, after a meal, or while drinking to be the most enjoyable cigarettes of the day. Some of the cigarettes you smoke are probably smoked out of habit. These are cigarettes that are smoked when there is not a strong craving and they are not all that pleasurable but they are smoked perhaps because others are smoking or simply absentmindedly when bored.

The following page provides an example of a structured diary that has been adapted for smoking. The first three columns are tracking information relevant to identifying situational triggers; time of day, place, and who you are with when you smoke. The last three columns all track information pertaining to your behavior in these situations. That is, whether you smoked, what your mood was, and the intensity of your craving. The focus of the intervention is on these particular aspects of the antecedents and behaviors associated with smoking. If you think you might benefit from adding an intervention aimed at thoughts and/or consequences then add this information to your diary. When you use your diary it is particularly important that you record each cigarette as you smoke it, even the cigarettes that you "borrow" from friends.

Before you begin, make enough copies of the smoking diary to get you through at least the first five weeks of the program (a one pack a day smoker needs 35 copies; a two pack a day smoker needs 42 copies; and a three pack a day smoker needs 49 copies). Success depends on keeping good records so it is important to make record keeping as convenient as possible. You probably want to get a notebook for your record sheets so that you can keep them all together. You can carry your record sheet with you (its easiest to fold it and keep it with your cigarettes) and at the end of the day put the completed record sheet in your notebook.

Smoking Diary

Name <u>Bill</u>

Date <u>9/16/87</u>

Time	Location	Who With?	Craving	Mood	Smoked
1. 6:05	bathroom	Alone	5	comatose	yes
2. 6:10	bathroom	Alone	4	tired	yes
3. 6:35	kitchen/coffee	Alone	2	relaxed	yes
4. 6:55	kitchen/talking	wife	1	happy	yes
5. 7:20	car/music	wife	2	happy	yes
6. 7:35	car/talking	wife	1	happy	yes
7. 8:05	smoke room	co-workers	2	energetic	yes
8. 10:00	smoke room	co-workers	5	irritable	yes
9. 12:00	lunch room	alone	5	hungry	yes
10. 12:20	lunch room	alone	3	relaxed	yes
11. 12:30	outside/talking	Jim & Gary	1	relaxed/happy	yes
12. 12:35	outside/talking	Jim & Gary	1	relaxed/happy	yes
13. 12:55	outside/talking	alone	3	apprehensive	yes
14. 2:30	smoke room	co-workers	4	tense	yes
15. 2:40	smoke room	co-workers	2	relieved	yes
16. 5:05	car/talking	wife	1	happy/up	yes
17. 5:15	car/thinking	wife	1	relaxed/happy	yes
18. 7:05	rec room/tv	alone	2	relaxed	yes
19. 9:30	kitchen/bills	alone	3	tense	yes
20. 9:45	kitchen/bills	wife	4	frustrated	yes
21. 9:55	kitchen/bills	alone	3	tired	yes
22. 10:30	bedroom/read	wife	2	relaxed/tired	yes

Total # of Cigarettes_____

Use a 1-5 scale to rate the intensity of your craving. 1=no noticeable craving to 5=intense craving

Smoking Diary

Name_____   Date_____

Time	Location	Who With?	Craving	Mood	Smoked

Total # of Cigarettes_____

Use a 1-5 scale to rate the intensity of your craving. 1=no noticeable craving to 5=intense craving

150

Treatment

Week One. The first week you simply want to record your smoking behavior in your smoking diary. Do not make any attempt to reduce your smoking this week. Your task for the week is to develop the habit of keeping good records. Your goal is to keep the smoking diary for at least 6 of the previous 7 days and to make your entries <u>at the time you smoked</u> at least 90% of the time. If you have succeeded at this you are ready to proceed. If not continue with the week one exercises until you have met these goals.

Week Two. Review your smoking diaries and look for patterns. Do you smoke more at night, on the weekends, when alone, when tense, etc? For each of the categories Location, Who With, and Mood from your diary, you will make three separate hierarchies of smoking desirability such that the top of each hierarchy is the cigarette(s) that is (are) most desirable and the bottom of the hierarchy are the least desirable of the cigarettes you smoke. The smoker from the sample diary created the three hierarchies on the following pages.

You have two goals in week two. The first goal is to reduce the number of cigarettes you smoke per day down to 20 or less by the end of the week. If you are a two pack a day smoker this means you should reduce by 3 the number of cigarettes smoked each day of the week to get from 40 to 19 (from the first of the week to the last would be 37, 34, 31, 28, 25, 22, and 19 cigarettes, respectively). Each night count out the number of cigarettes allotted for the next day. Again, you need to record each cigarette as you smoke it and record any cigarettes that you obtain from friends. Your second goal for this week is to eliminate all Level 5 smoking. For our example smoker Bill, this means he would not smoke in the rec room, in the presence of his wife (his wife is delighted), or when he is feeling energetic. This will probably be sufficient to bring the number of cigarettes smoked down to the desired level. If you are faithfully eliminating all level 5 smoking but your total number of cigarettes smoked remains too high, then eliminate those cigarettes which have a low craving intensity associated with them. If you are a lighter smoker to start with and are beginning the cessation program at about a pack per day make your goal 10 cigarettes by the end of the week. Whether you are an extremely heavy or light smoker you still want to set your goal for the first week at between 10-20 cigarettes. It is important that you not smoke in any level 5 situations even if you exceeded your goal for the day and feel like you have a couple of extra smokes coming to you. This is a stimulus control procedure. For it to work it is important to completely break the links between the situational cues associated with the level you are working on (in this case level 5) and smoking.

Hierarchies of Smoking Desirability
(Based on Bill's Smoking Diaries)

Location

Level 1 _____ Smoking Lounge at Work

Level 2 _____ Bathroom

Level 3 _____ Kitchen

Level 4 _____ Car

Level 5 _____ Rec Room

Who With

Level 1 _____ Alone

Level 2 _____ Co-workers

Level 3 _____ In-laws

Level 4 _____ Jim & Gary

Level 5 _____ Wife

Mood

Level 1 _____ Tense/Anxious

Level 2 _____ Irritable/Angry

Level 3 _____ Relaxed/Content

Level 4 _____ Happy

Level 5 _____ Energetic

Note. Higher levels reflect higher levels of smoking desirability

Hierarchies of Smoking Desirability

Location

Level 1_____

Level 2_____

Level 3_____

Level 4_____

Level 5_____

Who With

Level 1_____

Level 2_____

Level 3_____

Level 4_____

Level 5_____

Mood

Level 1_____

Level 2_____

Level 3_____

Level 4_____

Level 5_____

<u>Note</u>. Higher levels reflect higher levels of smoking desirability

Week Three. In week three your goal is to reduce the number of cigarettes smoked down to 10-15 per day by the end of the week and eliminate cigarettes in fourth level situations. By the end of the week you want to be a non smoker in all level 4 & 5 situations. During this week you want to develop and practice skills that will help you resist cravings now so that when you reach quit day you will already have experienced resisting the urge to smoke. Below are some things to try this week to prepare you for resisting cravings.

1. Postpone the first cigarette of the day and try to increase the delay each day of the week.
2. When you smoke, put your cigarette down between puffs.
3. When you are in a situation when you are allowed to smoke (level 3, 2 or 1) insert a time delay between when you first think you will have a smoke and when you actually get the cigarette out and light up.

Practicing these exercises will help break the chain of behaviors that lead to smoking. These exercises also provide you with repeated self-initiated experiences with cravings and resisting cravings. By the time you get to quit day you will have developed a multitude of strategies to resist cravings that will increase your confidence in your ability to succeed. The section later in this chapter on Coping with Cravings suggests some strategies for resisting cravings. Adapt these to your own situation and develop new strategies that work best for you.   The one thing you do not want to do, however, is to be a clock watcher. Keep yourself busy doing something else, work, play, relaxation exercise, whatever, but do not watch the clock. If after your self-imposed delay the urge has passed then forego that cigarette. As always, give yourself plenty of self-praise for delaying smoking and eliminating some smoking.

Week Four. By week's end you will be ready for total abstinence (we mean abstinence from cigarettes only; fortunately you will still be able to enjoy life's other pleasures).To prepare yourself for quit day your goal is to reduce the number of cigarettes smoked per day to 10 or less by the sixth day of the week. Refrain from smoking in all 3rd, 4th, and 5th level situations. In the middle of the week delete all 2nd level situations as well. By the end of the week you also want to be deleting some 1st level situations. On the 7th day of the week smoke five cigarettes or less.

Continue to practice all the delaying tactics that you started in week three. To help you move up your hierarchy during the week arrange to make smoking increasingly difficult and time consuming. Put your cigarettes and smoking accessories (ashtray, lighter, matches) far away from each other (different rooms of the house; difficult to reach cupboards etc.). Retrieve them when you smoke and put them back after each smoke. Make it time consuming to get a cigarette. For example put several rubber bands around the cigarette box, wrap your cigarettes up in tin foil, put the cigarettes in a bag or box and tape it shut. After you have smoked a cigarette, wrap the cigarettes back up again. To continue to break the chain of events associated with smoking, try holding the cigarette and smoking with the opposite hand.

Week Five. Congratulations!! Week five begins with Quit Day. If you have practiced the exercises in weeks 1-4 you are ready to be a non smoker. Do not delay and do not look back. You have worked hard to get to this point. Congratulate yourself, you have learned all the skills necessary to succeed.

Quit Day and Beyond

On the Day You Quit

* Remove as many of the cues which are associated with smoking in your immediate environment as possible.

> Throw away all your cigarettes and matches.
> Throw away your lighters and ashtrays.
> Wear clothes that have been thoroughly cleansed of the smell of smoke.
> Wash and or dry clean your other clothes to remove the smell of smoke.

* Keep very busy on the big day. Go to the movies, exercise, walk the dog. Just keep busy.
* Remind friends and family that this is your quit day and ask them to help you. You may want to review Chapter 11 on assertiveness in order to effectively solicit the type of social support you want
  from family and friends.

* If possible visit the dentist and have your teeth cleaned to get rid of tobacco stains. Pay attention to how nice they nice they look and resolve to keep them that way.

Immediately After Quitting

* Develop a clean fresh nonsmoking environment around yourself at home at work.

* Spend as much time as you can in places where smoking is not allowed like libraries, museums, and
  theaters

* Drink large quantities of water and fruit juice

* Have other objects ready, such as toothpicks, vegetable sticks, or lollipops that will help quench the craving both to have something in your mouth and that you can handle with your hands.

* Have other things available to do with your hands

Coping with Cravings

1. Think about why you quit. Go back to your list of reasons for quitting. Repeat these reasons while you practice your deep breathing exercise

2. Know when you are rationalizing. Its easy to rationalize your way back to smoking by saying things to yourself like "I'll just have one cigarette" "I have been good I'll reward myself with just one cigarette" or the first author's husband's "I will only smoke while we are on vacation"

3. Anticipate triggers and prepare to avoid them.

* keep your hands busy - doodle, knit type a letter
* avoid people who smoke; spend more time with nonsmoking friends
* find activities that are incompatible with smoking-exercise
* put something other than a cigarette in your mouth. Chew on carrots, celery, chew sugarless gum.
* Avoid places where smoking is permitted
* reduce your consumption of alcohol

4. Reward yourself for not smoking. Do not forget the power of self praise, which you can give yourself throughout the day when you resist cravings or avoid high risk situations.

5. Use positive thoughts.
6. Use deep breathing. Tell yourself to wait five minutes
7. Take advantage of your social support network

Relapse Prevention

Volumes have been written about relapse prevention for the smoker, alcohol and drug abuser, dieter, etc. There are three main "take home" points, things you really want to remember and act on, to ensure long term success with smoking cessation and controlled drinking.

1. A lapse is not a relapse. A term used often in relapse prevention is the Abstinence Violation Effect. This refers to the fact that often times when a person has a lapse, for example smokes a cigarette (or even a pack) after quitting for two weeks, they act as if that one lapse "ruins everything" and they return quickly to their pre intervention level of the behavior. That is, after violating their commitment to abstinence on one occasion people often misinterpret the act as a signal that they cannot really succeed. You need to be vigilant and not fall into this same trap. Do not let feeling guilty about one mistake lead to a string of other mistakes. To guard yourself against this phenomenon you must plan ahead to resist this type of thinking. You have the skills to recover from a lapse.

2. Avoid high risk situations and have a plan of action for those high risk situations that you cannot avoid. Do not go to the bar with your buddies if you know it will be almost impossible to refrain from drinking or smoking. To avoid being tempted plan ahead to participate in other activities with your friends where drinking and smoking would be incompatible behaviors, such as some physical exercise (racquetball, basketball). Go places with friends where smoking and/or drinking is not permitted (movies, museum etc).

3. Use the deep breathing exercise regularly in situations where you feel stressed. Practice the progressive muscle relaxation exercises. Generally work to keep your level of stress down. Feeling stressed is the primary reason give for relapse so guard against it with as many of the strategies covered in this workbook that apply to you.

Controlled Drinking

Changing your pattern of drinking behavior will utilize many of the same strategies reviewed for smoking cessation. As mentioned earlier in this chapter, self-management of drinking behavior described here is not aimed at the person with an alcohol dependency problem. In the textbook which accompanies this workbook four levels of drug use and abuse are described. This section of the workbook is aimed towards the person whose alcohol use falls in the range of drug misuse. If you suspect that your level of use falls in the categories of compulsive abuse or addiction (alcoholism) you may profit more from professional counseling. You might want to fill out the brief screening questionnaire presented below to assess whether your problems with alcohol are beyond the scope of this book.

Brief Michigan Alcohol Screening Test (B- MAST)

Honestly answer each question below by circling Yes or No

1. Do you feel you are a normal drinker?	Y N
2. Do friends or relatives think you are a normal drinker?	Y N
3. Have you ever attended a meeting of Alcoholics Anonymous (AA)?	Y N
4. Have you ever lost friends or girlfriends/boyfriends because of drinking?	Y N
5. Have you ever gotten into trouble at work because of drinking?	Y N
6. Have you ever neglected your obligations, your family, or your work for two or more days in a row because you were drinking?	Y N
7. Have you ever had delirium tremors (DTs), severe shaking, heard voices, or seen things that weren't there after heavy drinking?	Y N
8. Have your ever gone to anyone for help about your drinking?	Y N
9. Have you ever been in a hospital because of your drinking?	Y N
10. Have you ever been arrested for drunk driving or driving after drinking?	Y N

Scoring. Give yourself 2 points for No answers to items 1 and 2.
Give yourself 2 points for Yes answers to items 4, 5, 6, 7, 10
Give yourself 5 points for Yes answers to items 3, 8, 9.　　　**Total Score** ____

If your total score is six or greater you may want to consider professional help to help you change your drinking habits. If you feel that your drinking behavior is often a maladaptive way of coping with stress, and you scored less than a six, you can be optimistic that you can build a self management intervention for yourself that will allow you to control your drinking rather than having your drinking control you.

Self Assessment

As with the other interventions presented in this workbook, developing a structured diary that is tailored to your particular problem will be crucial to your success. Take a few minutes and think about those aspects of your drinking that you find problematic. Make a list. Below are a few examples of common situations in which people drink but wish they did not.

* Procrastination and drinking often go hand in hand. For example, you may procrastinate over some aversive/anxiety arousing task (e.g., studying) then drink to reduce the anxiety that procrastination produces, then regret drinking the anxiety away later when the task is still left undone.

* Another common situation where alcohol use becomes problematic is drinking to increase social acceptance. This applies both to the person who cannot say no when friends say "lets go party" and the person who drinks excessively in situations where they feel socially anxious.

* Not knowing when to say when and/or not turning over driving responsibilities to a designated driver or mass transit.

These are a few common examples of alcohol consumption causing problems that may strike a familiar chord with you. Complete the Situational Confidence Questionnaire on the following pages to get a better sense of the types of situations you may want to target for intervention. You need to list the aspects of your drinking that you find problematic and then use a structured diary to track the frequency and situational cues associated with the problem.

Intervention

Because the features of alcohol misuse that individuals seek to change are so diverse we do not recommend a single structured program. We do recommend that you draw on all the skills that you have learned to this point and put together an intervention plan, based on your self assessment information that is tailored to your problem. Below are some guidelines to help you develop an effective intervention.

1. Review your structured diary and your responses to the Situational Confidence Questionnaire and look for patterns in your behavior. Is problematic drinking associated with reducing negative emotions (anger, anxiety, tension). Does problematic drinking occur most often by yourself or with other people, during the week or weekend. Review your data and define your problem as a behavior in a situation.

2. Review Chapter 6 and identify interventions that you think are appropriate for what you have targeted for change.

3. Review your self assessment information and determine what other interventions covered in this workbook might be appropriate for you and review those chapters. For example if problematic drinking tends to occur in situations where people invite you to "party" with them you may want to review the chapter on assertiveness and build your request refusal skills. If problematic drinking occurs when you are angry go back to the chapter on reducing frustration and managing anger.

4. Write out your own plan for intervention including interventions for each aspect of the problem behavior you identify.

References and Additional Readings

Brown, T., O'Leary, T., & Barlow, D. *Generalized anxiety disorder*. In D. Barlow (Ed.), Clinical Handbook of Psychological Disorders. New York: Guilford Press.

Caudill, M.A. (1995). *Managing pain before it manages you*. New York, NY: The Guilford Press.

Charlesworth, E.A., & Nathan, R. G. (1982), *Stress management: a guide to wellness*. Houston, TX: Biobehavioral Press.

Curry, S., Gordon, J., & Marlatt, G.A. (1987). In Dickstein, D., Fiedler, J., & Passmore, M. (Eds.). *Breaking away: a guide to becoming a nonsmoker*. Seattle, WA: Group Health Cooperative of Puget Sound.

Davis, M. Eshelman, E.R., & McKay, M. (1988*). The relaxation and stress reduction workbook* (3rd ed.). Oakland, CA: New Harbinger Publications.

Dennett, D. (1988). *Consciousness explained*. New York, NY: Little Brown.

Dryden, W., & DiGiuseppe, R. (1990). *A primer on emotional therapy*. Champaign, IL: Research Press.

Ellis, A., & Greiger, R. (1977). *RET Handbook of rational emotive therapy*. New York, NY: Springer Publishing Company.

Ellis, A., & Harper, R. (1961). *A guide to rational living*. North Hollywood, CA: Wilshire Books.

Galassi, M.D., & Galassi, J.P. (1977). *Assert yourself: how to be your own person*. New York, NY: Human Sciences Press, Inc.

Greenberg, J.S. (1993). *Comprehensive stress management* (4th ed.). Dubuque, IA: William C. Brown Publishers.

Hanson, P.G. (1986). *The joy of stress*. New York, NY: Andrews and McNeal.

Jacobsen, E. (1929). *Progressive relaxation*. Chicago, IL: Uiversity of Chicago Press.

Kanfer, F.H., & Goldstein, A.P. (1980). *Helping people change* (2nd ed.) New York, NY: Pergamon Press.

Kelley, J.A. (1982*). Social-skills training: a practical guide to interventions*. New York, NY: Springer.

Kleinke, C.L. (1991). *Coping with life challenges*. Pacific Grove, CA: Brooks/Cole Publishing Company.

Lerner, H.G. (1985). *The dance of anger*. New York, NY: Harper & Row Publishers.

Levinson, J.C. (1990. *The ninty-minute hour*. New York, NY: E.P. Dutton.

Logue, A.W. (1995). *Self-control: waiting until tomorrow for what you want today*. Englewood

Cliffs, NJ: Prentice Hall.

Martin, G., & Pear, P. (1996). *Behavior modification: what it is and how to do it* (5th ed.). Englewood Cliffs, NJ: Prentice Hall.

Martin, G., & Pear, P. (1992). *Behavior modification: what it is and how to do it* (4th ed.). Englewood Cliffs, NJ: Prentice Hall.

Masters, W.H., & Johnston, V.E. (1966*). Human sexual response.* Boston: Little, Brown.

Masters, W.H., & Johnston, V.E. (1970). *Human sexual inadequacy.* Boston: Little, Brown.

Meichenbaum, D. (1985*). Stress inoculation training.* New York, NY: Pergamon Press.

Meyers, P., & Nance, D. (1991). *The upset book.* (2nd ed.). Wichita, KS: Mac Press.

Paul, K., & Jensen, M.P. (1987). *Multimethod assessment of chronic pain.* Oxford: Pergamon Press.

Pomerleau, O.F., & Pomerleau, C.S. (1977*). Break the smoking habit: a behavioral guide for giving up cigarettes.* Ann Arbor, MI: Behavioral Medicine Press.

Renshaw, D. (1995). *Seven weeks to better sex.* New York, NY: Dell Publishing.

Rice, P.L. (1992). *Stress and health* (2nd ed.). Pacific Grove, CA: Brooks/Cole Publishing Company.

Roger, P. (1988). *Behavioral relaxation training and assessment.* New York, NY: Pergamon Press.

Romas J.A., & Sharma, M. (1995). *Practice stress management: a comprehensive workbook for managing change and promoting health.* Boston: Allyn and Bacon.

Smith, J.C., (1993). Stress management for wellness: the 1-2-3 cope system. Englewood Cliffs, NJ: Prentice-Hall, Inc.

Walt, S. (1996). *Stress management for wellness* (3rd ed.). Fort Worth, TX: Harcourt Brace College Publishers.

Watson, D.L., & Tharp, R.G. (1993*). Self-directed behavior: self-modification for personal adjustment* (6th ed.). Pacific Grove, CA: Brooks/Cole Publishing Company.

Wolpe, J. (1958). *The practice of behavior therapy* (2nd. ed.). New York, NY: Pergamon Press.

Wolpe, J. (1990). *The practice of behavior therapy* (4th ed.) New York, NY: Pergamon Press.

Acknowledgments

Chapter 5

Are Your Emotions and Behaviors Helping You or Hurting You? Table from The RET Resource Book for Practitioners (1993). Reprinted by permission of the Albert Ellis Institute, 45 E. 65th St. New York, NY 10021.

How to Recognize Thinking That is Unhelpful, Distorted, or Irrational. Table from The RET Resource Book for Practitioners (1993). Reprinted by permission of the Albert Ellis Institute, 45 E. 65th St. New York, NY 10021.

Rational VS. Irrational Thoughts. Table from The RET Resource Book for Practitioners (1993). Reprinted by permission of the Albert Ellis Institute, 45 E. 65th St. New York, NY 10021.

Model of Rational Self-Management. Table from The RET Resource Book for Practitioners (1993). Reprinted by permission of the Albert Ellis Institute, 45 E. 65th St. New York, NY 10021.

Rational Self-Management Form. Table from The RET Resource Book for Practitioners (1993). Reprinted by permission of the Albert Ellis Institute, 45 E. 65th St. New York, NY 10021.

Chapter 11

Assertion Self-Assessment. Table from Galassi, M. & Galassi, J., Assert Yourself: How to be Your Own Person (1977). Reprinted by Permission of Human Sciences Press, Inc., a subsidiary of Plenum Publishing Corporation.

Chapter 12

Social Avoidance Stress Scale. Scale from Watson, D. & Friend, R., Measurement of Social-Evaluative Anxiety. Journal of Consulting and Clinical Psychology, 1969, 33,450. Reprinted by permission of the American Psychological Association.

Chapter 13

Time Management Scale. Scale from Charlesworth E. and Nathan, R., Stress Management: A comprehensive guide to wellness (1985). Reprinted by permission of Ballantine Trade, a subsidiary of Random House.

Chapter 16

Brief Michigan Alcoholism Screening Test. Test from Pokorny, A., Miller, B., Kaplan, H., The brief MAST: A shortened version of the Michigan Alcoholism Screening Test. American Journal of Psychiatry, 1972, 129, 342-345. Reprinted by permission of the American Psychiatric Association.